Cornel West Matters

Cornel West Matters

Politics, Violence, Racism, and Religion in America

Second Edition

Mahamadou Lamine Sagna

Translated from the French by Arlette Afagbegee

Worcester, Massachusetts

Original French-language edition: Violences, Racisme & Religions en Amerique: Cornel West, Une Pensée Rebelle, Un Philosophe Saturé de Blues et Imprégné de Jazz, by Mahamadou Lamine Sagna. Editions Karan, Paris, 2016.

Copyright © 2019, 2024 Mahamadou Lamine Sagna
First edition published 2019 by Karan Publishing Group
Second edition published 2024 by The WPI Press
The WPI Press
100 Institute Road
Worcester, MA 01609

Cataloging-in-Publication Data
Cornel West matters: politics, violence, racism, and religion in America / by Mahamadou Lamine Sagna; translated by Arlette Afagbegee; with a foreword by Stéphane Douailler

Includes bibliographical references and index.
ISBN: 978-1-965358-00-9 (paperback)
ISBN: 978-1-965358-04-7 (PDF)
ISBN: 978-1-965358-01-6 (epub)

1. African American philosophy. 2. West, Cornel—Philosophy. 3. West, Cornel—Political and social views. 4. Philosophy—Ethics and moral philosophy. 5. United States—Race relations.

DEDICATION

I dedicate this book

To my father and mother,

To Jean-Pierre Ndiaye, the Senegalese journalist and critic who brought about my first encounter with Cornel West.

To the late Professor Richard Brown, mentor, former professor at the University of Maryland, "le Juif New Yorker," who opened up my way to the United States and taught me what it means to be Jewish or Black in America. He left us too soon.

To all the students at Princeton University, American University of Nigeria, and WPI who took my classes.

Thanks to all the Masks. They know who they are.

Masks*! Oh Masks!

Black mask, red mask, you black and white masks,

Rectangular masks through whom the spirit breathes,

I greet you in silence!

And you too, Soundjata, my lion-headed ancestor.

CONTENTS

Foreword by Stéphane Douailler	xi
From My Encounter with Cornel West to the Writing of This Book	xv
Preface	xix
Introduction	xxxi
Part One: The Sources of Engagement	**1**
Cornel West, a Conceptual and Romantic Character	3
The Collusions between Religion and Politics	19
Violence in America	45
From Revolt to the Elaboration of Rebellious Thought	67
Part Two: Poetics, Philosophy, and Ethics of Engagement	**69**
Blues Thinking	71
Prophecy and Philosophy	99
Activism and the Poetics of Commitment	119
Cornel West: A Figure Worth Following	139
Post Scriptum	145
Acknowledgments	149
References	153
Index	157

FOREWORD

WHEN OLD SCHOOL SOCIALISM IS SWEPT UP IN JAM SESSIONS

Stéphane Douailler

For years, Mahamadou Lamine Sagna has retreated to solitary spaces where he has dedicated himself to writing a book, only emerging periodically as an unwavering supporter and facilitator of collective engagement in the inventive transformation of our societies. This book focuses entirely on the American philosopher Cornel West, and Mahamadou Lamine Sagna's aim is to pass it on to us. It is a very old gesture that Sagna revives for us with regard to Cornel West by telling us *Tolle, lege*! (Take it, and read it!)

It is indeed reading itself, solitary and silent reading, reading that welcomes in its heart the lapse via which we can somewhat distend our links with the pressing flows of life, as well as the resurgence of this lapse itself and the capacity to fit us into it, that take root here. However, to convey a *Tolle, lege!* to another, a childlike voice, boy or girl, or some "refrain that children used to sing while playing" no longer suffice (St. Augustine, Confessions VIII, 12). There must be a mediation that gets us to hear so that we listen to the song of other voices. We need, for example, West's oeuvre and Sagna's book, through which this mediation not only speaks to us but also about us. What can we hear about what America brings us?

All of the commentary patiently written by Sagna on West's works strives to take stock of this issue, which is simultaneously political and aesthetic. We know that there is a political theater in the United States of America that is quite similar to ours (in France). It even appears that these theaters resemble each other more and more without necessarily being aware of the direction in which this resemblance takes place. The plot is invariable. The will to power various markets, interested in the maintenance and development of an imperial militarism and an internal authoritarianism, creates an uneven playing field, consistently a winner with the cautious optimism or resigned pessimism of far-off echoes of possible relations of justice between people. Another way to say it, "*The plot remains unchanged. The drive for dominance by different markets, invested in upholding and expanding imperial militarism and internal authoritarianism, creates a lopsided landscape, where one side consistently emerges victorious, amidst the cautious hope or resigned despair of distant murmurs of potential just relations among people.*

Drawn up for this theater, the indefinitely replayed play obscures all others and feeds all despair. We should therefore be in search of all that this play doesn't bring to the performance, and it is to this end that Sagna submits West's oeuvre to an ambitious investigation. Old school socialism is one of West's starting points. In the 2016 American Democratic primaries, he notes with surprise the presence of socialism presented by Bernie Sander's candidacy. But also, more generally, West had begun dedicating himself to drafting his doctoral thesis, published in 1980 under the title The Ethical Dimensions of Marxist Thought, which opens for him a branched progeny, in a substantially different way.

In 1994, West's doctoral thesis culminates in a resounding publication entitled Race Matters, which addresses, one by one, all the themes of moral philosophy in the light of race and ethnic relations.

An accomplished critical performance on all fronts, Race Matters makes visible in the modes of enunciation of American citizenship, and in the devolution of its technological and economic possibilities, the lines that separate Whites and the Blacks, the history of violence, and denials of racial and racist domination.

A cartography of nihilisms emerges, which, at each junction, renews the gesture by which Blacks excluded from citizenship are brought back to their existence and humanity only for production. This critical gesture calls for another, and Sagna first identifies one of the sources in the proximity that West establishes with Jean-François Lyotard in 1987 at the International College of Philosophy. Sagna amplifies this proximity by putting West's works in resonance with those of Michel Foucault, Jacques Derrida, and Alain Badiou: What forms of emancipation can we discern and impel from the American map of domination?

The political and aesthetic fate of the invisible necessarily directs the gaze to scenes other than those of the restricted theater of Western democracies or the theaters of unhappy consciousness that fail to extricate themselves from it. It is for this reason that Sagna retakes West's oeuvre such that, like an echo of future works, starting with *Race Matters*, it engages reflection via two great "lines of escape": religion and music. Let us consider these lines successively.

In opening the chapter on the religious forms of emancipation, West acknowledges the political stakes represented by Martin Luther King's legacy. However, from West's point of view, one cannot consider that Barack Obama's election to the presidency of the United States of America alone could overwrite American political history, even though it is a major fact. King's legacy does not find its completion in the modes of enunciation of American citizenship and the elections. Far from being able to fit into the system of representations that governs the American state, the complexity of this legacy resides in a misunderstanding that is expressed in the history of Christianity: the opposition between Constantinian Christianity and prophetic Christianity.

Whatever pacts Christianity may choose to sign with the theo-political institution by subscribing or not to the pathologies of salvation found in the severity of morals and families and the prosperity of the great neoliberal trusts, there is the persistence of outside voices who have learned to denounce slavery, to demand women's vote, and to support civic and social movements and who open the way for enunciation through prophetic discourse. In these outside voices, there are outbreaks of violence that are not those of their various theo-political applications.

West's oeuvre and the commentary undertaken in Sagna's book make a considerable contribution. It is not only that the blues, a form of African American music, often destined for production, bears witness to capitalism's destruction of lives. The blues is also a response to the nihilisms that capitalism peddles and amplifies.

By endlessly writing a musical score of faith and hope in the song of suffering, West opens up the nihilistic times of domination to another time and way of inhabiting the world, when stasis, whether metaphor or paradox, contributes an indefinite (infinite) process of revelations.

The blues accomplishes this stasis for all music, for those acquainted with the blues already know in their versions of jazz, funk, soul, rap, and slam, which are not compromised by commodity fetishism or the sentimentalism of some evangelical action, that the blues is a means for liberation.

The blues is not one of these many forms of music, or just one form of music, and in this sense, it is neither just nor only music. It is, at the heart of capitalism and the misery it causes to rise in the world, that moment of suffering poison and finding a happy remedy through which feeling finds voice, rhythm, collective alternation of *temps* and *contretemps*. It is created in hopeful language for all and by all. To follow blues creations, to follow the minor partitions in which feeling becomes language, is not only to see how capitalism operates, but also to engage collectively in the prophetic paths that emancipate us.

Stéphane Douailler, Professor of Philosophy
University of Paris VIII, Saint Denis

FROM MY ENCOUNTER WITH CORNEL WEST TO THE WRITING OF THIS BOOK

My introduction to the enigmatic persona of Cornel West was orchestrated by journalist Jean-Pierre Ndiaye, a close associate of numerous African American artists and intellectuals during the late 1950s, particularly in the dynamic 60s and 70s.

In July of 2000, Jean-Pierre Ndiaye urged me to attend a conference at the Sorbonne featuring two African American intellectuals of "remarkable stature." Admittedly, I was hesitant, having just concluded an international colloquium on globalization that had drained my energy. Unfazed by my reluctance, Jean-Pierre, employing true African directness, insisted, "You don't have a choice; right now, you are going to the conference, and you will write a report for me." Thus, I acquiesced.

Arriving early, I found myself before the closed hall doors. A well-dressed couple, presumably the speakers, approached. The woman, devoid of pleasantries, ordered me to open the door. I responded with a reminder of common courtesy, asserting my identity as an academic attending the conference. It was in this moment that West, perhaps overhearing our exchange, approached and introduced himself.

Engaging in conversation, West inquired about my background and activities. This dialogue persisted for about twenty minutes, during which I mentioned my upcoming visit to the University of Maryland College Park in the United States as a visiting professor.

As we entered the conference hall, filling with members of the African American community in Paris, West's companion, also the moderator, ignored my request to speak. West intervened, insisting that I be the last audience member to address the conference. Post-session, he handed me his card, urging me to contact him upon my arrival in the United States.

I reported the conference to Jean-Pierre, thanking him for introducing me to the charismatic orator and profound philosopher, West. What struck me most about his talk was the insightful parallel he drew between Plato's allegory of the cave and the dim atmospheres of American bars.

Weeks later, while in Maryland, I consulted my mentor, the late Professor Richard Brown, about West. The response was unequivocal, likening him to Deleuze or Guattari, emphasizing his brilliance. I shared West's card with friends, sparking surprise and delight. Attempts to contact West proved futile, and I eventually moved on. Two years later, at Princeton University, I unexpectedly crossed paths with West again, marking another remarkable encounter.

Over the next ten years, I closely observed and engaged in extensive discussions and co-teaching sessions with West. Beyond his profound appreciation for intellectual and cultural works across eras and continents, I was captivated by his "love of others."

West is a people person. Accompanying him reveals a plethora of familiar faces greeted by name. His affinity for personal connections is exemplified by an encounter that inspired the title of one of his books, born out of a spontaneous meeting with musician Bob Dylan.

This book, a product of a decade-long reflection since my initial encounter, aims to capture the vitality and joy of life embodied by Cornel West. Despite challenges, I strive for authenticity and truth in portraying this extraordinary individual.

The writing journey began a decade after that first meeting, on Princeton University's secluded campus, and continued in the serene Norman countryside of France. The choice of Normandy, guided by intuition, invokes memories of verdant Casamance, my birthplace. As I delve into West's life and thinking, my surroundings echo with the songs and colors of my native land, evoking a blend of joy and melancholy. The narrative unfolds against the backdrop of Africa, the "Grand Brazier," an imagery fraught with poignant reflections on the state of my homeland.

PREFACE

UNRAVELING CORNEL WEST

The previous edition of this book emphasized that Cornel West, who is often on the fringes of the mainstream, does not settle for giving a voice to the vulnerable, but also challenges paradigms and opportunities for cohabiting to build a better world. This new edition further depicts his engagement and vision of a better world in which the voices of the most vulnerable are heard.

At a time when violence and racism wreak increasing havoc in America, it is important for me to write a book about a philosopher whose complex thinking deals with the world's and America's contradictions across several eras. Even with all the intellectual and media debates about the unfolding crises, there is so little wisdom on what is truly driving these forces and on how to move America forward.

With the announcement of his candidacy in the 2024 U.S. presidential campaign, it has become essential to update this book, dedicated to this unique author who explores the social, cultural, and intellectual foundations that characterize him. West, philosopher, activist, and prominent intellectual of our time, has a singular voice that transcends national boundaries and speaks to the contemporary world.

West is a familiar voice on religious, political, and racial issues in America and the world, but his philosophical sources often are not well identified. He stakes out iconoclastic positions that can confuse and confound his admirers and critics alike. West can put the reader or listener in a spiral in which time and space are confused.

In this book I am taking a fresh look at West's body of work in an attempt to better understand his dialectical approach and the social and political dynamics that exist in America.

At a time when economic globalization is steadily being shaped by proponents of a rampant neoliberalism, West's analyses of inequality, new forms of nihilism, and political, racial, and religious violence are increasingly relevant. For West, neoliberalism is an inequality-generating force that threatens harmonious coexistence within society. In the face of the relentless onslaught of neoliberalism, whose unbridled quest for profit prevails, West is convinced that society's most vulnerable souls must be afforded special attention and protection by the state. He sees the role of the state as crucial to reducing social disparities and providing a safety net for the most disadvantaged.

The reader of this book may wonder what can be said that West himself has not already said. My humble objective is to unravel the spiral and to reflect critically about West's pursuit of the truth.

West has remarkable insight into the mechanisms of violence and the anthropological stakes of domination within America's political, economic, and religious systems. He believes that what undermines coexistence in the United States—the development of market fundamentalism, aggressive militarism, and growing authoritarianism—also resonates internationally. His work invites deep reflection on contemporary challenges while offering crucial perspectives on building a more just and equitable world. His universalist perspective resonates powerfully in today's global context. His thinking encompasses a global vision that transcends national boundaries. His writing and speeches highlight the profound consequences of the social, cultural, and economic divide that affects the United States and many other parts of the world.

Some of his thoughts may help to analyze burning issues; others may be considered old-fashioned, but as a sociologist, all seem important to me in understanding the condition of humanity in the American political landscape.

An example is West's seemingly contradictory attitude toward President Obama. He campaigned for Obama in 2008, then he attacked him viciously for his handling of the global economic crisis, but then he agreed with him on Cuba and Iran and approved his statement in the wake of the racist killings in North Carolina.

Here's another example: In the 2015 Democratic Party presidential primaries, West supported social democrat Bernie Sanders against Hillary Clinton, whom he critiqued as a member of the neoliberal establishment. During the US presidential election, he confessed that he preferred the Clintonian "neoliberal disaster" to Donald Trump, whom he described as a "neo-fascist catastrophe." West doesn't just reserve his attacks for the national political class, he also denounces the ideological, moral, and intellectual blindness of some of the leaders of the African American community. He accuses the latter of betraying or even destroying the humanist heritage of forefathers such as W.E.B. Dubois, Martin Luther King, Jr., and Malcolm X.

Why does he seek to show, *urbi et orbi*, the incoherence of his fellow citizens' opinions and behavior in the world and in the United States? Why is this African American philosopher always on the lookout for the truth, running the risk of seeming contradictory and being censored by all sides of the American political spectrum? How did this philosopher, who claims to be imbued with the essence of blues and jazz, forge his ideas? How did he acquire the analytical tools needed to grasp the lives of our society's "invisible" members?

From classics such as Plato and Sartre to the Frankfurt School theorists, as well as African and African American writers, West explores a wide range of authors who have scrutinized issues of justice and the struggle against injustice. This intellectual diversity reflects the depth of his thinking and the scope of his commitment to social justice.

By denouncing the political elite, including those within the African American community, and by exhorting America's youth not to believe in this plutocratic elite, he reinforces the impression that he seeks to subvert them.

To better understand such postures and behaviors, we should turn to the Greek philosopher Socrates who West admires and often quotes. Socrates opposed both those who defined themselves as wise (a kind of aristocracy that claimed exclusive possession of knowledge) and Sophists, who claimed to be able to teach the whole world in exchange for remuneration. According to Plato, Socrates is the first philosopher because he desires wisdom itself more than he desires to appear wise to others. Perhaps this is the Socratic posture that West seeks to embody.

During his trial, Socrates was accused of rejecting the state-sanctioned gods, of introducing new deities, and of corrupting the youth. Although West has not undergone an official trial, certain American circles accuse him of rejecting the gods of capitalism (the market and the so-called legitimacy of American military power), of introducing new divinities (historical figures, notably forgotten African Americans), of being compassionate toward and standing in solidarity with the outcast, and of subverting the youth by his artistic and intellectual practices. Socrates inhabits West!

West is certainly well acquainted with the political reality of his contemporaries, but whether he plays with it or pretends to ignore it is a double feint. He philosophizes in the manner of Socrates, because let us remember that, for Socrates, to "know" is to know that we do not know, which corresponds to humility and therefore to a moral position and code of ethics.

With an extraordinary mastery of dialectics, and clear frank rhetoric, West is consistent in at least one regard—we can always depend on him to issue sharp criticism of American leadership. In the American collective narrative, the fantasy of the American "dream" is sacred, but West speaks of it as a nightmare. And while some people in power ignore certain historically marginalized demographics and their practices, West puts them at the center, as recourse to "re-humanize" America.

He plunges into the oceans of poverty to search the wreckage lying underneath for evidence of injustice, and then brings it to the surface. In this regard, West's thought is oceanic. Starting with the Atlantic slave trade that enslaved his ancestors and with the tools of Atlantic (European) philosophy, he elaborates his thinking and proposes the construction of intellectual bridges among the continents, especially America, Africa, and Europe. This is a great and fundamentally optimistic ambition despite the critical veneer. This assertion based on meticulous work first implies the need for critical analysis and handling the poverty indices and for the dissension around their historicity and their framing.

Like geologists who observe and study lava springing from long-dormant volcanoes, he analyzes and processes the signs of poverty in their historical and environmental context in order to then propose just policies.

In the American world where the poor and the weak are most often criminalized, West is a rare intellectual who addresses issues using atypical approaches. For him, if philosophy is the search for truth, marginalized places serve as a powerful locus for philosophical insights to emerge. Yet, in the field of academia this is a countercurrent approach. It is an offbeat rhythm West embodies.

To better understand his thinking one should consider the offbeat rhythm that has characterized African American tragicomedy: pain and joy. Writing in a language punctuated by pain and hope, this philosopher who called himself blues saturated and jazz infected seeks to grapple with American capitalism, which he deems treacherous. He frees himself from academic constraints and the cultural and political burdens in a bid to critique the attitudes of the leaders, stereotypes, and the politics of the United States.

I began writing this book in the spring of 2012. It is the result of a lengthy effort of criticism and synthesis of some thirty works written or cowritten by West. In preparation, I read or reread philosophical, sociological, anthropological, and literary works he quotes often. I spent dozens of hours listening to African American music he references: jazz, blues, soul, R&B, funk, rap, and so on. It is a book that inhabited me. Some may wonder why I did this–why combine reading and listening to expose his thinking?

I did this, because in order to understand West, it was important to immerse myself not only in the content of his analytical thought, but also in the experience of the cultural forces that shaped his thought. The seminal idea of West's work is to highlight the marginalized individual, the neglected. He makes the emergence of the individual a central theme of his work. From this point of view, it is important to immerse oneself in the culture in which he seeks to grasp the truth. He loudly and precisely proclaims what the marginalized populations lack: freedom and justice.

Philosopher, literary critic, and political commentator, West appears as a unique entity within the American philosophical space. For him, the presence or absence of individuals in the economic and political field must not lead to a rejection of their humanity or the truths they carry.

To better broadcast this moral philosophy that inscribes the "nonexistent," West uses the media and intellectual forums. In fact, as Marc Abeles writes, "Cornel West, an unconventional intellectual, grabs the public stage like a jam-session space" where he makes his work and his life a practice of freedom.[1]

By intervening in these different spaces, he shows not only his multiple affiliations, but also reveals experiences that he had internalized and recomposed during his career. He appears often on important TV shows (CNN, Fox News, Tavis Smiley, etc.), his name is in the credits of box office films (*Matrix 2* and *3*), and his statements to the press garner a lot of public attention.

This intellectual who is so visible, coming from groups traditionally considered invisible, treats social issues, political conflicts, and race relations in the United States with both passion and rationality.

---
[1] Cornel West, *Tragicomique Amérique* (Paris: Payot, 2005), p. 9.

He claims, rightly or wrongly, to speak on behalf of the invisible. At a time when the United States was led by a "Black" president, is such a posture not antithetic? Why would West, the intellectual who, by his charisma, has an undeniable presence on the public scene, insist on the issue of visibility and invisibility? Doesn't West's rekindling of this debate at that moment appear out of step?

It should be made clear from the outset that, for West, the call-and-response form that constitutes the rhythm of the blues helps us to understand the condition of the "invisible" at different times in history. Thus, in the 1920s, Du Bois, highlighting the problem of visibility/invisibility, spoke about the veil and the challenges of the color lines (the questioning of the dividing line between Blacks and Whites) in the twentieth century.

In the 1950s, Ralph Ellison and Frantz Fanon[2] wrote extensively on this issue of Blacks in the West. Admittedly, the issue of visibility and invisibility is not expressed in the same way, but with the resurgence of racial or even racist violence, this debate is central. West extends and moves this debate into other fields. Drawing on the works of black American thinkers, religious leaders and artists, as well as those of *La Négritude* and European philosophers, he seeks to show how identities are recomposed in an open world.

He invites us to think about places, especially marginalized places, to better analyze the contradictions and find solutions to overcome them. These marginalized places are fertile ground from which to address issues of freedom and human dignity. Going to these places is tantamount to excluding oneself from the mainstream, from the norm. But for him, it is important to occupy these spaces where one can study and ponder the complex challenges of America that are, *inter alia*, the relations of interdependence and identity, exclusion, and complementarity between individuals.

These places that he refers to as "chocolate cities" (where Blacks and Latinos live) are places where one can grasp the forms of symbolic reproductions, cultural mixes, social compartmentalization

---

[2] Frantz Fanon, *Black Skin, White Masks* (New York: Grove Press, 1967).

and de-compartmentalization, or even bases of innovations. However, according to him, in order to be able to work in these places, one must not only respect the humanity of those who are there, but also seek to promote living together.

Thus, very often, he expresses opinions that testify to the suffering, the cry, the anger, the fury, but also the joy and happiness of these marginalized populations.

When asked if this immersion in the neighborhoods of African American populations is likely to lead to a kind of separatism, he responds that, on the contrary, it will lead to an assessment of the dynamics, the living conditions and practices of composite entities. He chooses his multifaceted interventions to progress, inasmuch as it is possible for him, into the turf of knowledge and action.

These places allow him to unveil the logic of movements between social and cultural practices and ideas buried in mental structures. They also permit him to go beyond the misleading appearances of ideologies and to understand the foundations of cultural and social expressions. To do this, he does not limit himself to discourses and narratives expounded by the "voiceless"; he confronts them with their own attitudes.

He performs the exegetical, holistic and interactive task, because to understand the blues of the African American people today is to hear the gasp of the "nonexistent," the ancestors. And this gasp is often through musical and religious channels. But, although it is soaked with African American music, it has a subversive and constructive relationship with religious beliefs. Although he uses religion as a tool of emancipation, he is wary of this same religion. He distinguishes the "Constantinian Christianity," which is geared toward power and money, from prophetic Christianity, which is based on the search for peace, love, justice, and freedom.

West places religion within the field of philosophy. Religion, through prophetic voices such as those of Martin Luther King, denounced slavery, called for women's suffrage, and supported liberation movements. As such, it is an object of study for philosophy.

These are prophecies that call for melodies in minor key which, for their favored performance, use the blues and its dialectical springs. Thus in the fields of misery, the blues, soul, and rap songs follow minor scales within the rhythms that alternate in time and space. In other words, in African American culture, his voice drives new dynamics for expressions of the soul, feelings and sensations of his community. By allowing himself to be caught in America's contradictions and by making blues and religion the beacons of his approach, West equips himself with the tools to describe the life of an entire people.

In a society where racial, social, and economic tensions are so prevalent, it is not easy to bare the feelings and resentments of a group without being locked into a category. In the political, cultural, social, and American university environment, he runs the risk of being outcast or despised. But for him, the game is worthwhile because it entails telling the truth about inconsistencies and injustices and working for a more just society. West's work allows for the discussion, analysis, and confrontation of contradictory opinions, ideas, and theses.

Continuing the African American tradition, he speaks to all his interlocutors by memorizing their names immediately preceded by "Brother" or "Sister." But why are these expressions that signify soul brothers and sisters under certain conditions, and in others that signify kinship links, so important to him?

For West, love is fundamental for society. According to him, even adversaries have to be loved. The purpose of this book is threefold: (1) It is to show how this intellectual invests the different sites of truth (love, art, science, society); (2) it is to present his thinking about America's history, society, and politics; (3) it is to show how his philosophy converses with the European philosophy of the twentieth and twenty-first centuries, and to lay out how West uses African American art to philosophize. There is arguably one other intent that undergirds all three of these, which is to show how he tries to demand acknowledgement and assertion of humanity for people to whom it is often denied.

Delivering to the world a bouquet of joy and sorrow, hope and despair, emotion and lucidity, I capture West as both object and subject. Molded by adversity, West as a former athlete does not hesitate to cross borders considered impassable by his fellow citizens. In a Coltranian[3] posture, he whispers truths that emanate from deep pains, and he asks others to express their own.

Through his work, he reveals the essential influence of music, particularly jazz and the blues, on his intellectual approach. For him, jazz people and blues people, as democratic figures, carry within them a tradition guided by humility and creativity. It is in the footsteps of these musicians, through their mesmerizing rhythms and enchanting melodies, that West finds his inspiration, acknowledging with profound serenity the greatness of every human being around him.

West is a person who brews and interweaves so many ideas: a researcher who moves between worlds at a jarring pace, a jazz-infected and blues-saturated philosopher who repeats "when I have the blues, I sing the blues," an enigmatic and iconoclastic intellectual who often leaves his audience in a swirl of contradictory ideas and emotion. But one guarantee is that he will not leave anyone indifferent! In times like these, with the challenges faced not only by American society but also around the globe, we must all join West in the battle against indifference.

"WESTIAN" GLOSSARY

chocolate cities: Neighborhoods comprising predominantly African American and Latino populations.

Constantinian Christianity: At the service of power, money, and empires. This expression refers to Constantine, the Roman emperor who legalized Christianity and chose to lean on the Church to bolster his power.

nihilism: For West, nihilism is considering others as nothing. In the best-case scenario, it is understanding the existence of the

---

[3] Reference to the great jazz musician John Coltrane.

other at the margins as a marker of distance. He sees three forms of nihilism: *religious nihilism*, *paternalistic nihilism*, and *sentimental nihilism*.

religious nihilism: Consists of not tolerating any contradictory point of view.
paternalistic nihilism: Does not speak to people sincerely and seeks to corrupt;
sentimental nihilism: From a compassionate posture, evades reality and distorts truth.
prophetic Christianity: Based on a constant quest for justice, peace, and love. It is founded on the Jewish prophetic traditions (Moses, Elijah, Jeremiah, etc.) conveyed by Martin Luther King, Jr.
tragicomedy: The ability to laugh at the tragedies and dramas experienced in order to endure the pain.
Socratization: Critical reason and dialogue.
vanilla suburbs: Neighborhoods with a high concentration of White inhabitants.

INTRODUCTION

> I live with fear and anxiety, with the absurdity of the human condition, through the prism of the cross.
>
> *Cornel West*

The way America portrays itself today is written about extensively. The contradictions of its political and economic systems are very difficult to decipher from the outside. From California to New York, by way of Florida and Missouri, we are simultaneously witnessing the blossoming of technological innovations and the explosion of violence. While constant technological changes generate hope, the social climates in which they take place incur deep frustrations. The system that produces these scientific and technological advances is unable to contain, to stem, the permanence of social dramas. Isn't it surprising that America is offering such great opportunities while at the same time creating as many bottlenecks?

On the one hand, there is the unprecedented development of technological means in America that is transforming the world and generating optimism, and on the other, the resurgence of racial and even racist violence and police brutality that destroy lives and cause a lasting loss of trust.

For some citizens, America's economic and democratic horizons are brightening, and for others, they are darkening. In these conditions, how does one decipher the contradictions of this fascinating and intriguing country? What is the logic underpinning these contradictions? How does one catch sight of a beam of light in this darkness?

Faced with this sensitive opposition (shadow and light, black and white), some claim that it is impossible to put an end to racism. On the contrary, others think that America has entered the post-racial era, especially with the election of Barack Obama. What is in fact the case?

To see how we can get out of this impasse, I summon the thoughts of a singular author: Cornel West. But why West? How is his thinking significant in the analysis of the contemporary American political debate? What is the knot that clinches the different aspects of his analyses of America's contradictions?

West is an enigmatic figure. An atypical teacher and activist, whose style is both rippling and incisive, he is very active in social movements, be they religious, artistic, or political. In America, where social relations between "racial" groups often amount to glances, West chooses religious, artistic, and political spaces as places of truth. He shows that if these places that bring together Black and White populations are spaces of tension and of ethical and aesthetic confrontations, they are also where all the possibilities arise. Between these populations, there is both proximity and distance.

From symmetrical positions, Black and White talk to one other; the distance separating these populations is also the place where the work of each is in resonance with the other's gaze. From this distrustful or even defiant gaze, it is possible to think about the conditions of living together.

If living together is the search for a harmonious life, the harmony between Black and White must take into account their contrasts but also the inherent contradictions of these categories. West seeks to explore the conditions of understanding and justice in America. He is interested in the ideologies that generate the social and cultural practices of different racial, religious, and artistic groups in their specificities and intersections.

From the analysis of the capitalist system, he also shows how Americans' living conditions cannot be isolated from those of the world's other peoples. Of course, America alone cannot bear the responsibility for the fragmentation of a torn world, but it is the symbolic unity of the world's contradictions. The discrepancies between facts and political discourse within the United States are also those that we see elsewhere. We observe in the world that which corrupts living together in America: the development of market fundamentalism, aggressive militarism, and rising authoritarianism.

West then asks himself the following question: How can one aspire to a democratic life when capitalism introduces injustice and inequality within the very collective? Though this questioning is not new, it refreshes the twentieth-century European philosophical debate in novel terms: What are the possibilities of social and political inclusion of "the Being" the capitalist system considers "nonexistent" while this same system claims to be democratic?

In thus refreshing the twentieth-century European philosophical debate in triumphant modern America, West invites us to a reflexive approach to "the Being"—philosophy's enigma par excellence—which seems to be understood only in its opposition with "being" (all things that are), even if it is conceded that without the former (the Being), the latter (being) would not manifest itself.

West shows how, in accordance with the times and across different domains, the process of American capitalism's theoretical and practical construction has developed within and outside America, considering Beings merely as "beings." Whether through technology or the management of human resources, in capitalism, we use technique[4] to establish nihilism; the other is worthless.

From this reflection, which reveals a fundamental dimension of his work, one gets the sense that West first seeks to pinpoint these "nonexistent beings" in multiple spaces, then to inscribe them, to trace their humanity, to record their individual stories in collective memory.

---

[4] The technique is in essence nihilistic since it only considers the Being (human being) as an observable being, meaning it uses human being as a raw material.

He also takes precautions to ensure that his work is not distorted and that his analyses of exclusion are not reclaimed by nihilist powers. As we will see, this reflection on nihilism and otherness is of major importance because it allows him to philosophize between existence and being; we cannot reduce economic inexistence to non-being.

He shows how the social construction of the Being and the non-Being, one of the essential characteristics of White supremacist ideology, still simmers in the background of American capitalism. Thus, today, the new forms of racist violence are only resumptions of White supremacist ideology. To illustrate his point, he sifts through the political, economic, and religious discourses, as well as their interconnections, showing that the American elite fashion themselves and their speech generally with lies and the omission or even the denial of this White supremacist ideology.

America, in its perpetual, forward-looking flight, can legitimately promote democracy and find both opportunities to overcome conflicts and harmonious solutions only if it carries out its self-examination, for the critical reasoning he calls Socratic reasoning is a democratic zest: "The Socratic love of wisdom holds not only that the unexamined life is not worth living (Apology 38a), but also that to be human and a democratic citizen requires that one must have the courage to think critically for oneself" (*Tragicomique Amérique*, p. 222).

To be able to talk about democracy, America must first accept that supremacist violence constitutes its social and political life. It must then take stock of the atrocities it has sown inside and outside its borders. It is this self-criticism or awareness of its imperial aggressions that will enable it to grasp the hatred it provokes in the world and within its borders.

West adds, "This love of wisdom is perennial pursuit into the dark corners of one's own soul, the night alleys of one's society, and the back roads of the world in order to grasp the deep truths about one's soul, society and world."[5] According to him, Socratic questioning is all the more relevant nowadays that "our business elites

---

[5] Cornel West, *Democracy Matters* (New York, Penguin, 2004), p. 208.

have cloaked themselves in the rhetoric of the unfettered free market and of the inevitable juggernaut of corporate globalization, justifying an obscene exacerbation of wealth inequality" (*Democracy Matters*, p. 204).

In sum, Socratic questioning must lead us to engagement instead of confining us to reasoning that prevents us from hearing what resonates within society. For him, philosophy, like any type of knowledge, must be at the service of the community. But he does not stop at theoretical analysis; he explores and gets involved on different fronts to make the voices of the poor heard because coming from a population that has suffered all forms of violence, he himself is witness to injustices. This shared suffering leads to revolt, but he remains aware that resentment and the experience of injustice, when not channeled toward humanism, always end in blind confrontation.

In his eyes, fighting for justice certainly starts with individual experiences, but it is ultimately working for universal truth and good. It is therefore a permanent struggle for equality among Beings. Justice is always a work in progress; it is never completed. He is committed to political, religious, social, cultural, artistic, and academic matters. In all these areas, he places himself at the borders, he says, to try to attach the scattered fragments of a right and just world. The search for justice is what underpins his work. Social, religious, and artistic movements enriched by the contributions of African Americans are privileged places to reflect upon justice, peace, and harmony.

West's work can be read on several levels: sociological, anthropological, economic, and philosophical. Some might find this architecture complicated and highly intellectually constructed, but is the figure himself not complex?

West appears as the epitome of both America's academic elite and minority groups. Through this dual membership, he occupies privileged intellectual and media spaces to study America and examine this society's complex challenges. From his social position, he reveals the experiences he has internalized, recomposed, and assembled throughout his social, cultural, and intellectual trajectories. He is a leader of opinions who represents these minorities in perpetual reconstruction in their acts, elocution, and constantly transient spaces. Moreover, West's philosophical stance and political commitment can only be understood if one takes into account the cultural and religious values that have nourished his life. Religion and art, especially music, represent a basis for him to develop liberating and solidary thought.

Having had a religious Baptist upbringing, he performs a biblical exegesis to show how religion can serve as a bulwark against downward spirals. For example, for West, Martin Luther King Jr.'s prophetic Christianity is a means of fighting against injustice and corruption and helps to strengthen peace and democracy. The prophetic word leads the way to love of wisdom.

He connects this religious prophecy to African American music to show how it can be used to confront suffering and strengthen "American democracy." This approach leads to a reflexive approach, because to reveal my Being I must try to grasp the "Being" of the other, and to reveal their Being, they must recognize mine.

Apart from King, in his intellectual genealogy West cites great African American writers such as Ralph Ellison, Amiri Baraka (Leroy Jones), Toni Morrison, James Baldwin, and Richard Wright, who all express the blues of the invisible with precision and lyricism. But he does not stop there! He bases his philosophy on an interpretative discourse or context of religion that at the same time harkens back to all the configurations and meanings proper to the Black struggle.

Whether it is through African American artistic, religious, or social experiences, he shows that not only is it possible to identify the conditions for enunciating and bringing about emancipation in America and the world, but it is also possible to access the truth of Beings. This approach, which is one of the modes of re-appropriating the figure of the outcast Black, present or absent, is also a way of appreciating the humanity of all Beings, including that of the outcast. This is to say that West develops a geometrical thought pattern that institutes other spaces and openings of time through its circulation.

To work on the oeuvre and the figure of West is not only to seek to inscribe the understanding of his work and his actions at different levels of American social life, but also to try to extend his original, philosophical concepts to the rest of the world. To better decipher the thoughts of an author as sophisticated as West, we have organized the work in two parts: part one the sources of his engagement; part two on the philosophy and poetics of his engagement.

In part one, we are interested in the imprints he leaves, which still mark the multiple instances of the American public space in which he operates. We will show how West exploits the cultural and linguistic resources of his community *ad libitum*, and how he uses the apparatus of the academic world to philosophize. In particular, we will see how he treats the sedimentary discourses in America's political, economic, and religious system to identify the mechanisms of violence and the anthropological issues of domination.

In part two, we will show how this fervent activist constructs and elaborates his thinking from pragmatism, religious prophecy, African American art, and emancipation struggles. It is from this reflection that we can contemplate, promote, and organize the brother- and sisterhood, the individual freedom, and the equality of citizens to the highest degree. In fact, the question he asks himself is how to formulate the procedures capable of founding solidarity among Beings. In answering this question, he develops a poetics of engagement from art and religion that values the humanity of Beings.

By way of conclusion, we will show how he encourages dialogue by exposing himself to criticism. But isn't that philosophizing: seeking to grasp the truth?

PART ONE

The Sources of Engagement

A philosopher and specialist in religion, Cornel West has served as professor of religion and African American history at Union Theological Seminary, Yale, Princeton, and Harvard. An influential member of America's intellectual community, West is also an influential member of the Black community. But what is the foundation of this intellectual stance?

To become acquainted with the sources of engagement of the enigmatic figure that is West, we have traced his social and intellectual trajectories. The work and approach of this African American who grew up during the civil rights movement are marked by two major axes:

- The religious anchoring of the Black struggle
- The Vietnam War

These issues urge him to simultaneously reflect upon the scars of violence, the place of religion, and the genesis of democracy in America—a very delicate approach, for he must carefully lift, one by one, the stones that constitute the markers of misunderstanding and at the same time show that the political fight must be substantial and materialize in the social body. To do this, he indicates the ways.

He first emphasizes the need to recognize the wounds inflicted upon and sustained by populations. This makes it possible to render the "invisible" visible, that is, to recognize them as subjects possessing rights. That said, if the conditions of the possibility of living together go through the recognition of the outcast's humanity, they also traverse the deconstruction of the systems that establish this injustice. But to contemplate justice is to have the principle of equality as a horizon. It is in the dialectics of the visible and the invisible that one can think about the conditions of living together.

Thus, at first, we will see how he makes his cultural and social trajectories a place of philosophy. Above all, we will show how, starting from the dialectic of the values of his emotional environment and the methods and concepts acquired at school, he elaborates his thoughts and forges his intellectual approach and his ethics.

Then, we will show how, through detailed, documented descriptions, and a coherent and fluid analysis, he addresses the issue of the collision of religion and politics. He shares with us his thrills, his anxieties, his hopes. He shows that in American society, so strongly impregnated with religious beliefs, the contradictions in the attitudes and behaviors of some also reflect, in part, the contradictions of others. To get out of this vice, he proposes a new reading of religion.

Finally, we will demonstrate how he plunges into the history of the United States to reveal the political system's inconsistencies and show how the all-powerful American state recurrently plays at, and with, democracy and freedom in America and in the world. So, to understand the issue of America's violence is to look at how past atrocities of White supremacy such as the genocide of Native Americans and slavery are connected to current national and imperial economic policies.

Citing Alexis de Tocqueville in his book De la démocratie en Amérique, West recalls that with the mixture of imperial practices and social conflicts, America produces a new form of despotic democracy, a democracy perverted by demagogy. With this perversion of the system leading workers nowadays to take up residence in professional know-how, in work discipline, without, however, being able to live decently from the fruits of their labor, West sums up the necessity for the intellectual to take up this struggle alongside workers.

1

CORNEL WEST, A CONCEPTUAL AND ROMANTIC CHARACTER

> I am a Bluesman moving through a blues-soaked America, a blues-soaked world, a planet where catastrophe and celebration, joy and pain, sit side by side. I am a jazz saturated Bluesman.
>
> *Cornel West*

The fecundity of Cornel West's work undoubtedly resides in the fruit of his astute analyses of the multiple religious and artistic experiences of African Americans. West is what Gilles Deleuze calls both a *romantic and conceptual persona*.[6] To say it another way "*Cornel West would be both the representative figure of what Gilles calls a romantic persona and a conceptual persona.*" Let us remember that for Deleuze, the conceptual persona is a power of concepts, while the romantic or literary figure is firstly a power of affects.

With respect to West's conceptual persona, we can say that he appears and reappears today as a subject who seeks to think politics, love, art, and science. As a romantic persona, he is a subject who can be reconstructed in different narratives. In this second case, our text apparently focuses solely on the person of West himself. In fact, he allows us to explore the marginal figures of the citizen, the activist, or the militant.

---

[6] Gilles Deleuze and Félix Guattari, *What is Philosophy?* (New York: Columbia University Press, 1994).

Recourse to Cornel West's conceptual persona makes it possible to grasp the lineage and intellectual productions of a little-known America; recourse to his romantic persona allows us to set up very practical pegging systems with American cultural references.

This approach makes it possible to see the validity of theories in a social space where the freedom of human beings is often denied. He intervenes in several sites and leaves his tracks. In these conditions, how does one figure out this character and give a clear appreciation of his work? How does one go about it when the tracks are numerous? How does one gather all the different threads of his life into a knot? How does one find someone who appears and disappears within the limits of our field of vision? In this chapter's first section, we will trace the life of this jazz-soaked bluesman. In a second section, we will show how he uses African American cultural, social, and religious experiences to philosophize.

IN THE FOOTSTEPS OF A JAZZ-SATURATED BLUESMAN

It is no easy feat to pin down a character as complex as West. He appears alternately, and sometimes simultaneously, in political, cultural, and academic fields. While failing to define him, we have some tags at our disposal to locate him. To do this, we will use methods proposed by Michel Foucault, Jacques Derrida, and Alain Badiou.

Pinpointing Cornel West

West grew up in a family of civil rights activists who instilled in him the necessity of promoting rights. His parents taught him the tragic history of Blacks. Growing up, he is gradually influenced by the sermons of great Black preachers and by African American music (jazz, soul, blues, rap, etc.) In middle and high school, he tries by all means to give real meaning to the ideas he has received from his community, including by seeking to include the history and culture of African Americans in his school's programs.

Educated in the greatest American universities, Harvard and Princeton, West attempts to deconstruct the culture of domination and furthermore to inscribe the "nonexistent" in the political, academic, and economic fields. To do so, he does not hesitate to dive into the American imaginary and reality to address symbolism. In these conditions, how does one go about pinpointing this atypical intellectual, who goes against the established norms of the American academic institution and even throws it off balance?

Indeed, he travels in different universes with varying degrees of intensity (e.g., family, neighborhood, university market, etc.). In these worlds, where he temporarily appears and disappears, one perceives only part of his Being. He positions himself at the borders of the political and academic fields to be able to slip into other places. West is therefore a multifaceted Being. But, as Badiou (2008) and Foucault (1969) suggest, from the notion of discursive imposition, one can capture the generic multiple Being West.

Let us remember that, for Foucault, the experience of the world is always an experience of discursive imposition, that is to say, in each "world," Beings are marked by discourse, including in their bodies. According to Badiou, it is from the transcendence of a "world" that is the relationship characterizing this world and that one can grasp how the being is shown as a Being, that is, "as he is there, so as he occurs in this world, or appears beneath the horizon of a determined world."[7]

In the world of American politics, which is characterized by a political opposition between right and left, West provides us with clues with which to pinpoint him. His harsh criticism of the Republican policies of Ronald Reagan and Presidents Bush (senior and junior), his strained relations with Democratic Presidents Bill Clinton and Barack Obama, and his proximity to Bernie Sanders, enable us to place him to the left of the American left. The dilemma is that, very often, the multiple being West, who is marked by egalitarian political discourse close to the Marxist analysis on equality, is also very marked by religion. He takes quite puzzling religious positions for someone who is of the left. In doing so, he is a vanishing point in the

---

[7] Alain Badiou, *Le Petit Panthéon Portatif [The Portable Small Pantheon]* (Paris: La Fabrique Éditions, 2008).

American intellectual and political space. He is in and out of place. But how does one localize this vanishing point?

One of the possible tracks is given to us by Jacques Derrida's deconstruction approach. Derrida proposes a cartographic method. For him, even if we can never precisely demarcate the vanishing point, we can track the target to get closer to the place where it vanishes. To achieve this, Badiou proposes we use the image of the hunter. But beware, warns Badiou, this image of the hunter should not lead us to think we are hunters. Indeed, unlike the hunter who seeks to seize, to kill the animal, for Derrida and Badiou, it is just a question of being able to locate the target. It is like an inverted chase: What must be grasped is not the animal for slaughter, but the one who appears in and eludes our field of vision. Unlike hunters who wants the animal to stop so they can kill it, Derrida does not want the "hunted" to stop. He hopes that the escape and the pursuit will not cease. With West, the pursuit is constant.

We find him at a place where he has appeared and from which he has disappeared. Knowing that we cannot grasp him because he systematically appears in and disappears from our field of vision, to be able to locate him as precisely as possible, we must try to get as close as possible to this place. As West is in and out of our field of vision, let's examine his tracks and his shadow.

At a vanishing point of American intelligentsia, West applies de facto to American society the approach we have applied to his figure. Indeed, being himself a multiple being, he also perceives others as multiple beings, that is, beings whose totality we cannot know. Aware that he cannot grasp all the meanings of human practices—there is always a vanishing point—West seeks to get as close as possible to the outcasts, to touch them to better grasp their Being. Remember, Cornel West is obsessed with the disappearance of the Being. He likes to navigate the social environment of the poor, the excluded, to inquire into reality in order to reveal truth. To deconstruct the process of dehumanization in America, he seeks to locate "worlds" (cultural, economic, social, political, etc.) in different places, the spaces and vanishing points of American history and sociology.

But how does he build his methodology? How does he manage to produce his work in a language that is simultaneously philosophical, poetic, and prophetic? To answer this question, we will look at some biographical and bibliographic elements.

SOME BIOGRAPHICAL POINTS OF REFERENCE

From Childhood to Maturity

Cornel Ronald West was born on July 2, 1953, in Tulsa, Oklahoma, a state in which several Black communities established themselves in the early twentieth century to escape racism in the southern states. These Blacks had developed a thriving economy until the riots of 1921. The state of Oklahoma, especially the city of Tulsa, is steeped in history for African Americans.

The son of a teacher and a military base employee, West learned the history of the Black struggle at a very young age. His father, employed at a military base, took him along to the various African American marches for civil rights so that he could see how the members of his community combine agonic (struggles for their survival) and symbolic (to give meaning to their life) activities. The young West grew up in a context of racial segregation and saw this system as a dehumanizing enterprise.

The inequalities of American society gave him "nausea." Indeed, he heard the speeches of Black leaders stressing that the Black experience is not just an experience of contingency, or, in other words, that of Beings without justification in the same way as objects of the world. He was deeply affected by the injustice of this system extoled by White supremacists. While his thoughts on this apartheid system (Jim Crow) had yet to form, what preoccupied the young West boils down to a requirement: how to first ensure the development of the mind. His entry into high school coincided with the legal end to racial segregation, yet racial inequalities persisted. It was in high school, in the midst of the Black struggle for equality, that young West asked the school administration to offer American African studies.

After high school, he matriculated at Harvard College, where he graduated *magna cum laude* in three years, instead of four, obtaining a bachelor's degree in near Eastern languages and civilization. In his autobiography, he recounts how he struggled to graduate early to allow his parents to save money on his schooling.

It must be stressed that, at Harvard, West had the philosopher John Rawls, *inter alia*, as a professor. The latter, having himself fought in the Second World War and lived through the Vietnam War, considers it more necessary than ever to set up a justice system that will allow for a harmonious social life. For Rawls, the struggle for civil rights is a philosophy of justice and *contractualism*. His professor's teachings on the philosophy of justice and ethics are the bases from which the young West sought to articulate individual freedom and social solidarity. But, unlike the teacher, the former pupil later showed that to achieve real justice, it is important to take into account residues, in other words, that which by definition any procedure leaves outside of itself. For West, one cannot transform conceptions of justice without upsetting the whole structure of the political and social system.

West joined Princeton University to pursue postgraduate studies. In 1979, he obtained his doctorate in philosophy under the direction of Sheldon Wolin. The latter, a specialist in political philosophy, taught him the importance of temporality and timelessness in the analysis of the political creature, which he applies both to the analysis of the Greeks' classical problems and to the contemporary problems of modern organization. He says that at Princeton, he also experienced the influence of Richard Rorty's pragmatic approach to philosophy. He acquainted himself with Ralph Waldo Emerson's and Herman Melville's thoughts on pragmatism. In doing so, he managed to reconcile the religious and traditional teachings he received from his community with those of philosophy. He says that his method and his ideal of freedom embrace the prophetic witness of love (*Tragicomique Amérique*, p. 185). As we can see, this way of combining religious faith with critical philosophical questioning is not common, which makes him a non-conformist intellectual, an atypical academic.

THE ATYPICAL ACADEMIC

Always dressed in black and white, West appears as an eccentric within the walls of academia. Some people may see a narcissistic tendency in this self-differentiating clothing, others a simple way of provoking prescribed codes. In any case, it is an affirmation of identity that undertakes a subversive game with the rules. This aesthetic and spiritual posture certainly demands recognition, but it also indicates a break in the vision that one has of the teacher on the one hand and of the representation that is given of the Black man in America on the other.

Shadow and Light

By playing with the rules while respecting certain standards, this posture echoes what could be called Black dandyism. This posture is not new in the African American community. From W.E.B. du Bois to Malcolm X and Martin Luther King Jr., African Americans in general, and religious and intellectual leaders in particular, have always distinguished themselves through their sartorial elegance and sophistication. In fact, though in England the style called dandyism was associated with contempt for the codes of *savoir vivre*, among French romantics this sartorial elegance was considered the reflection of an aesthetic and spiritual sense. Baudelaire says of dandies,

> these beings [the dandies] have no other status but that of cultivating the idea of beauty in their own persons, of satisfying their passions, of feeling and thinking. Thus they possess, to their hearts' content, and to a vast degree, both time and money, without which fantasy, reduced to the state of ephemeral reverie, can scarcely be translated into action.[8]

Although it seems legitimate to say Black leaders intend for these outfits to show elegance and refinement, for West, always wearing a

---

[8] Charles Baudelaire, ed., *Le peintre de la vie modern* (Paris: Mille et une nuits, 2010).

black suit with a white shirt is to emphasize a classic representation in American society.

With respect to the Black/White opposition, it is not wrong to say that these outfits also express something subtler, the search for a border between these two extreme colors: the chiaroscuro. The black-white ensemble allows him not to be locked in a frame, and like Becket's (1951) black-gray ensemble, to merge the closed and the open, to discreetly place himself in an ideal position to better see, while escaping the gaze of others, he can thus appear in and disappear from their field of vision. For West, sartorial elegance is a way of marking one's time and space with one's footprint and representing a cultural heritage. Whether on the academic, political, or media scene, he is observant and observed, deliberately putting himself in the limelight. Behind his tinted glasses, it looks as though he's trying to escape scrutiny. This posture is a way for him to invite the other to overcome visible contradictions by plunging into the imaginary and the real. In the marks of the black/white, visible/invisible opposition, he names America in a specific and immanent manner.

It is by taking into account the differences between the experiences lived by Black populations and the discourse produced about them that one can trace axes that allow one to free oneself from the discourse of hatred and revenge that constitute abysses of thought. To hope for a better life and to avoid obstacles to a harmonious democratic life, he shifts his analysis of violence to the field of religion.

For West, the becoming of the Being and that of thought are intrinsically linked; they lend structure to themselves and to social life—the quest for a reformulated democracy that cross truth and action. Let us say with Marc Abeles,

> it is as though the course of this academic intellectual condensed the most glaring contradictions that characterize the great, world-renowned academic institutions, simultaneously jealous of the reputation of seriousness that makes them famous, and fierce as soon as it is about

recognizing success when it surpasses the Areopagus of authorized specialists. Because he is one of the most provocative and well-known American media intellectuals and one of the most prestigious representatives of academic excellence, Cornel West is indeed this unclassifiable person who upsets established conventions. *(Tragicomique Amérique, 2005, Préface de Marc Abeles).*

CORNEL WEST'S RESEARCH AGENDAS

In 1980, West published his dissertation under the title *The Ethical Dimensions of Marxist Thought*. After this publication, he joined the Union Theological Seminary as an assistant professor. In 1984, Yale University's Divinity School offered him a professorship in American history. He used this platform to teach revolutionary texts that push students to question their ideologies. In the university community, he was involved with the workers. On Yale's campus, for example, he protested with trade unionists against apartheid in South Africa, which resulted in his arrest.

In retaliation for his union involvement, the administration at Yale retained him during the spring of 1987, though he had obtained a position as visiting professor in France. This constraint forced him to make weekly trips to teach both at Yale and in Paris. It should be noted that it was in Paris, during his stay at the College International de Philosophie, that Cornel West approached Lyotard, postmodern philosopher who had already prefaced the book he had coauthored with John Rajchman, *Post-Analytic Philosophy*.

In the fall of 1987, West returned to Princeton, where he becomes professor of religion and director of the African American Studies program. In collaboration with different partners, Toni Morrison among others, he revitalized this program.

He left Princeton in 1994 to join Harvard's Department of African American Studies. The number of students enrolled in his classes was so large that he had about fifty assistants; he was obliged to give his classes in a church due to the amphitheater not having enough seats for all the students.

In 1998, he was finally appointed to the prestigious position of university professor at Harvard University (the holders of this position are very few). Unlike other professors, the university professors report directly to university presidents and have particular advantages in terms of income and power.

Later, in 2001, West was at the center of a controversy with Harvard University's new president, Lawrence Summers. Summers accused him of spending too much time on politics and not enough on academic activities because West made a hip-hop album entitled *Sketches of My Culture*. Following this quarrel, he summarily left Harvard University in 2002 and returned to Princeton University, where he remained until his retirement in 2012. He then joined Union Theological, where he began his teaching career.

In 2003, he played the role of councilor in the *Matrix Reloaded* and *Matrix Revolutions* films. For the release of the *Matrix* DVD box set, he recorded philosophical commentaries related to the problems of the Wachowski brothers' film work.

As we can see, it is difficult to assign a place and a status to this versatile character West. In seeking to be himself and to vanish into the other (the nonexistent), West employs seduction. But what happens when one wants to remain oneself, that is, to keep one's own identity, and to take on becoming the other? What happens to you when you think you embody the essence of a whole society and at the same time keep your own singularity?

The answers to these questions would be very long. It can be said, however, that it is from a dialectic between a radical otherness and his own identity that West tries to assert his being. He uses African American cultural, social, and religious experiences. For twenty-five years, while teaching at the most prestigious universities, West taught courses in American prisons. He took part in various political protests, including Occupy Wall Street. He also used multiple conceptual tools of pragmatism and continental philosophy to develop his thinking. Despite the heterogeneity of his approaches and sources of influence, there is a common thread in West's thinking. We will show this thread by reviewing some elements of his work.

RELIGION AND PHILOSOPHY WITH CORNEL WEST

In most of his work, West seeks to introduce prophecy, a religious category, in the domain of philosophy. In his memoir, *Brother West: Living and Loving Out Loud*, he recounts how it was during the civil rights protests that he was exposed to the aggressive theology of Black Baptist preachers whose voices were softened by Martin Luther King. West will say that despite the significant, though marginal, presence of Islam, African Americans remain marked by the Protestant Church: "Preachers are the only members of the elite who are aware of the everyday problems of simple people in their community. They are better placed than other personalities to gain the trust and respect of their peers."[9]

It is undoubtedly this closeness to the leaders of the Baptist Church, renowned for their defense of outcasts, that explain West's future positions in favor of the civil rights movement and the defense of the poor. Indeed, for him, churches and Baptist preachers in particular are always the first to sound the alarm, to warn of a social situation and the risks involved. The sermons of these churchmen, like the tones and sounds of the blues, not only teach about the cycles of happiness and misfortune, but also give hope and expectation to society.

But West draws our attention to the fact that, just like all religious ideologies, this Protestantism is politically ambiguous: It has two poles, one ecclesiastical and conservative, the other prophetic and progressive. We will come back to this distinction. Reading these few biographical and bibliographic elements, we see that there are two Wests, as Louis Althusser would say: the young and the wise. On the one hand, the young West is drawn to prophetic discourse and, on the other, to pragmatic teaching, the wise West seeks to synthesize both.

Having received a traditional religious education, this preacher's grandson naturally uses the living language of his community to reveal the truth. For him, it is not about using speech to replace the

---

[9] Cornel West, *Brother West: Living and Loving Out Loud. A Memoir*, 2nd ed. (New York: Smiley Books, 2010).

written word, nor the opposite, but rather about using speech and writing in a complementary way to avoid loss of meaning and to inscribe unspoken truths in books.

In fact, for this unparalleled speaker trained in the school of religion and art, mastery of the "art of speaking by which life is given to facts and gestures," is a necessity for abandoned and neglected populations.[10] It allows them to resurrect and to retransmit the song of martyred and forgotten lands and flesh. In his lectures, this great orator always tries to show his physical presence and intellectual posture through staging. He often says that he does not express himself simply to please (aesthetics), but also to speak truth and goodness (ethics).

BLUES AND PHILOSOPHY

In his philosophical lectures, West often illustrates his thought not only with bibliographical references, but also sometimes with musicological and discographic references. He manages to organize his ideas as much with the works of Plato, Aristotle, Hegel, and Sartre as with the songs of James Brown, Marvin Gaye, Bessie Smith, and the music of jazzmen like Miles Davis and John Coltrane.

The blues and jazz offer possibilities of escape from the cycle of violence. He says the blues is a musical genre that allows one to keep hope alive, despite the suffering experienced (*Brother West: Living and Loving Out Loud*, p. 201). By singing, the bluesman relieves his anguish and transforms it into strength. Blues is a tragicomic procedure inherited from African Americans that allows people to be hopeful in spite of suffering.

In other words, the blues is a subliminal (or compensatory) means through which people experiencing a negation of their humanity find, in music and laughter, pathways out of exclusion, despair, and tension, or even laugh at their situation. Thus, put into perspective, the blues as a psychic state is not an exclusively American

---

[10] Djibril Tamsir Niane, *Soundjata ou l'épopée mandingue* (Paris: Présence Africaine, 1960).

experience. It can be extended to the rest of the world. Blues is a feeling that all beings experience and is a way for all of the world's peoples, especially for the "wretched of the Earth" as Frantz Fanon would say, to escape violence.

This dimension of African American music has already been articulated by several twentieth-century authors, among them Marguerite Yourcenar. In her admirable anthology *Fleuve profond, sombre rivière* (*Deep River, Dark River*), Yourcenar reveals to us how African Americans in the southern states transform Anglo-Saxon words and express their dreams, their humanity, their revolt, their deep sorrow and suffering, and their simple joys with admirable intensity and simplicity through Negro spiritual texts and music. Yourcenar insists that Negro spirituals are not just entertainment for lovers of exotic films and music; they are above all an authentic poetic genre. Through Negro spirituals, African Americans use African rhythms, religious texts, and symbols as comforts that keep them from drowning in the deep and dark rivers of misery and despair.

Like Yourcenar, West shows that African American art shows both the unspeakable and inexpressible and grasps the mélange of joy and despair. This is very visible and comprehensible in the cries and voices of blues singers in particular.

Living to the rhythms of jazz and to the tones of the blues, West manages to evaluate, at his own pace, and with the required tone, the forms of humanism and barbarism, as evidenced by his assertion that he became and remains a philosopher trained in the school of the bluesman because the blues singer comes from Black Christian culture and has a different recounting of history. West equates his deep and husky voice with that of the blues singer.

By inscribing his approach in a constant sinusoidal movement (ascending-descending) back and forth between the universe of capitalism's "elected" and that of those which capitalism excludes, he jostles the obsolete codes of the system. With a multifaceted style that is part philosopher, part pamphleteer, part prophet, and part activist or artist, West is a difficult figure to define. To be or not to be sums up the "tension" in which the bluesman finds himself caught up, a position from which West approaches life and seeks to reflect upon the world.

West defines himself as a bluesman soaked in jazz. It is undoubtedly from this sensitivity that he dares to think of proven and viable forms of democratic experiences, because if democracy is above all a matter of culture, lifestyle, ethics, and worldview, then the practices, aesthetics, style, and universe of blues and jazz can nourish the democratic model, a matrix of sonorous universes in which each voice in the orchestra, the group, and the collective expresses itself in its singularity and exceptionality.

West's intellectual, prophetic, and artistic posture reflects his singular life but also invites a general reflection on the condition of Blacks in America. He navigates between sound and symbol and image and speech to capture and connect energies, he says. This approach is also part of an insatiable pursuit of arms and a search for conceptual fulcrums to mark out paths that will lead to the foundation of a new democracy in which no one will be left by the wayside.

Insofar as his reflections and his practices feed on the artistic and religious practices of the invisible, he transmits and translates an African American genealogy from this ancestral presence that is very often forgotten. His positions express and bear witness to the suffering, the cry, the anger, the fury, but also the joy and the happiness of all the wretched of the Earth. His work is not limited to the contribution of African American art, especially blues. It also touches upon the religious prophecy of Martin Luther King and the pragmatism of American philosophy. While religious prophecy allows him to grasp the questions of existential and social freedom, pragmatism allows him to reflect on the practical conditions needed for setting an emancipation agenda.

By combining prophecy with pragmatism, West addresses intersections between racial and even racist questions of power, justice, and freedom. By integrating the prophetic tradition of Christian thought, Marxist social criticism, and Black liberation theology in this manner, West manages to construct a theoretical framework that allows him to elaborate a concept: prophetic pragmatism. One can say that West seeks to slip some prophecies into the field of philosophy.

In short, the biography of West is the biography of an entire people. Through the diffracted bodies, sensations, impulses, and contradictions of American society, one can grasp the forms borrowed by humanism and barbarism.

As you can see, it is not easy to classify this conceptual and romantic figure of West, but from the political, academic, and social worlds we have been able to pinpoint him and the anchor points of his thought. He develops his thought and lets himself be caught in his social and cultural incursions and in his academic practices. In the next chapter, we will see how he deals with and analyzes facts, discourse, and practices in America. For West, violence is constitutive of the social and political life of an America that claims to be the queen of democracy, a country where we observe a lot of injustice and violence.

Indeed, if to deconstruct is to pinpoint the vanishing point, to pinpoint a vanishing point is to consider a transcendence of the "world" where the elements of truth appear more or less intensely. If we manage to grasp some elements of truth, there are others that escape us because the Being always has a multiple identity. Yet it is not because certain elements of his identity escape us that they do not exist.

West seeks the vanishing points of outcasts' identities in the leftovers and dregs of society. However, he does not stop at social structures. He is also interested in mental structures. He shows how the system of domination and exclusion operates and settles in society through the collision between religion and politics. In the next chapter, we will see how he carries out this deconstruction.

2
THE COLLUSIONS BETWEEN RELIGION AND POLITICS

I do not want to be numbered among those who sold their souls for a mess of pottage—who surrendered their democratic Christian identity for a comfortable place at the table of the American empire, while, like Lazarus, the least of these cried out and I was too intoxicated with worldly power and might to hear, beckon, and heed their cries (*Tragicomique Amérique*, p. 185).

How do religion and politics, which are different vectors and do not have the same properties, employ particular procedures to objectify, incorporate, and legitimize the same set of differential disparities (differences in practices, unequal distribution of capital, etc.)? How do they think they can generalize into the world their local, particular, rooted, and singular experiences? By what processes do religion and politics, which are in two different regimes or orders, succeed in eliminating their borders to slip toward each other? How do these two different structures that do not have the same language come to think in the same paradigm? How do they manage to translate or even to convert into each other?

It is from the abstract notion of universalism that this politico-religious alliance seeks to generalize its values. For this alliance, Christianity and capitalism defend universal values. Their affirmed "universal" values are opposed to the "values of others," which are considered sectarian, erroneous, or even "anti-values." By claiming that their truths are universal, these politicians and

Christians in America, who are concerned with money and power, grant themselves the responsibility of carrying and spreading their values throughout the world, including by force. But, concretely, what does this declared universalism hide?

West shows that the alliance of these political and religious elites, who have different values and projects, can only reside in contradictions. With each party thinking that its "universalism" must supplant others, their hegemonic tendencies lead to shocks. This is the reality regarding certain conflicts between imperial governments and religious groups.

Indeed, religion and empire, each claiming its universalism, can only be at odds unless they reach agreements to share the "pie." With a great sense of investment, each party plays the other's game to satisfy its aims. They blur the boundaries between the religious and the secular. Politicians summon God to legitimize their practices, and religious groups use their power to position themselves as financial intermediaries. According to West, they are all the more likely to do so in America as they know how to use the beliefs that constitute part of the cultural capital incorporated by all Americans. And the politico-religious order present in America is only a dramaturgical remake of American capitalism's founding events.

To show this, he submits the classificatory logic of this alliance to a series of critiques, the most important of which is deconstruction. It is ambiguity or, if you prefer, blending that allows capitalist forces and certain religious currents to slip toward each other, to get along, to legitimize each other. This manipulation must be deconstructed by showing that the cumulative nature of capitalism on the one hand, and the attached religious vision of a superior, theological principle on the other, can only function under a process of exclusion.

THE AMBIGUOUS ADVENTURE OF RELIGION AND POLITICS

For us to better understand the foundations and stakes of this alliance, West invites us, as we have already stated, to carry out a sort of archeology of politico-religious capitalism in America

(*Prophetic Reflections, Notes on Race and Power in America*, 1993). By analyzing the historical relations between religion and politics, he shows us the limits of this alliance both from the point of view of democracy and that of religion itself.

He shows that today, as in the past, certain religions have signed pacts with temporal powers, not for humanist purposes, but rather to profit from imperial discoveries and expansions; those who have opposed this design have been marginalized, cast out, vilified, and slandered. For him, if the analysis of the alliance between these two powers takes on a particular accent today in America, it is because this configuration joins market value and spiritual value.

In this context, how can one lay bare this strategy of crossing political and religious borders? West is careful to point out that there are mainly two types of Christianity: Constantinian Christianity and prophetic Christianity. Prophetic Christianity is based on a constant search for justice, while Constantinian Christianity is at the service of empires.

Constantinian Christianity and Prophetic Christianity

For West, the prophetic Christianity borne by Martin Luther King is a far cry from Constantinian Christianity. Prophetic Christianity is based on Jewish and Christian prophetic traditions (Moses, Elijah, Jeremiah, etc.) and enables the fight for justice everywhere in the world, for all minorities (Jewish, Kurdish, Latin American, etc.).

As for Constantinian Christianity, the term refers to the Roman Emperor Constantine, who legalized Christianity and chose to rely on the Church to bolster his power. These two types of Christianity, whether local or not, extending more or less into the "greater whole" that is the world, are not of the same order. They clash radically, and moreover, when one takes flight, the other reacts viscerally. Constantinian Christianity not only hinders the democratic process in America, but also hampers the development of peace in the world, in alliance with other "imperialist" religious currents. If prophetic Christianity appears as the anti-capitalist side of Christianity in America, Constantinian Christianity appears as the religious side of American capitalism. However, West says,

> Ironically, the powerful political presence of imperial Christians today is inspired by the success of the democratic Christian-led movement of Martin Luther King Jr. The worldly engagement of King's civil rights movement encouraged Constantinian Christians to become more organized and to partner with the power elites of the American empire. (*Democracy Matters*, p. 164)

For West, much attention needs to be paid to Constantinian Christianity because its strength lies in its ability to shape and convey demands and mechanisms of domination over individuals so that these individuals act implicitly and unconsciously. This surveillance is all the more necessary and urgent as Constantinian Christianity is constantly being constructed and rebuilt in the economic, social, and cultural dynamics of American capitalism.

At the national level, this collusion between politics and religion leads to dysfunction in democratic procedures and processes. The alliance between "the throne and the altar" is all the more harmful to America in that it brings about existential problems and makes it difficult for people to live together. It causes people to withdraw into themselves.

> The rise of Constantinian Christianity in America went hand in hand with the Republican Party's realignment of American politics—with their use of racially coded issues (busing, crime, affirmative action, welfare) to appeal to southern conservatives and urban white centrists. (*Democracy Matters*, p. 164)

It marginalizes all citizens who disagree with official policy.

At the international level, this politico-religious alliance, which endows churches and politicians with an all-powerful role to the detriment of democratic decision making, leads not only to crises of confidence and scandals, but also plunges America and the world in a precarious and uncertain climate.

THE COLLUSIONS BETWEEN RELIGION AND POLITICS 23

The junction between Constantinian Christianity and capitalism must therefore be deciphered from their respective ideological matrices. Like capitalism, which values the culture of consumption, promotion, and publicity, Constantinian Christianity glorifies material gain and narcissistic pleasure, retreating to narrowly individual concerns.

These unscrupulous politico-religious elite use this consumer culture to satisfy their ends. The circulation of money and material goods makes it possible to abolish the borders, which are supposed to separate the domain of religious beliefs from the political domain. In the same way, the structural organization of Constantinian Christianity is hierarchical and legitimized by power and property. The agreement between religious and political powers can only bring about a confusion of roles between religion and politics. Indeed, blending the general frameworks of social relations' functioning and organization disorients citizens and counters instances of sovereignty.

A Short History of Constantinian Christianity and Prophetic Christianity

West notes that the battle between Constantinian Christians and prophetic Christians dates back to the first centuries of the Christian movement's emergence from Judaism. The integration of Christianity in the Roman Empire certainly cloaked the Emperor Constantine in respectability, but the latter stripped this religion of Jesus' prophetic fervor. West writes,

> Until Constantine convert to Christianity in AD 312 and decriminalized it with the Edict of Milan in 313, and his successor Theodosius I made Christianity the official religion of the empire, the Christian movement had been viciously persecuted by the imperial Romans, primarily because the growing popularity of the Christian message of humility, and of equality among men, was understood as a threat to Roman imperial rule. (*Tragicomique Amérique*, p. 161)

He adds,

> Jesus was so brutally executed by the Roman empire—crucifixion being the Empire's most horrific and terrifying tactic of punishing offenders to its rule—precisely because his preaching of the coming of the kingdom of God was seen by the Roman Empire as dangerously subversive of the authoritarianism and militarism of the Roman state. Ironically, Jesus's message of love and justice promoted a separation of his prophetic witness from Caesar authority "render unto Caesar what is Caesar's. (*Democracy Matters*, pp. 147–149)

Roman imperialism was so greedy for power that it could not tolerate the growing popularity of Christian sects. However, not being able to stop the progress of this religion, the strategy of the empire was to seize upon it, in particular through the conversion of Constantine. Thus, the collusion between Church and state, from which Jews in particular suffered so much, was institutionalized. As the state corrupts the Church, religious rhetoric justifies imperial goals. So, West says, "the corruption of a faith fundamentally based on tolerance and compassion by the strong arm of imperial authoritarianism invested Christianity with an insidious schizophrenia with which it has been battling ever since" (*Democracy Matters*, p. 148). In other words, the blending of Church and state led to the worst exactions and barbaric crusades against Jews and Muslims, the horrors of the Inquisition, and doctrinaire bigotry against women, Blacks, Native Americans, and other groups.

According to West, Puritanism, the first American branch of Christianity, is the heir of this religious schizophrenia. On the one hand, these early American Christians waged an anti-imperialist struggle against the British Empire, and on the other, they participated in the imperialist subjugation of Amerindians. They first waged a struggle for the triumph of democracy, and then turned on the natives with the British Empire's arbitrariness and authoritarianism, against which they had fought. White Puritanism therefore simultaneously constructed and deconstructed the democratic process. But by signing pacts with political power, this Constantinian branch of Christianity not only justified slavery and approved policies of inequality toward women, but it also weakened this religion's universalist dimension. Today, it is these same conservative Christians who demand state-funded religious schools and carry out anti-abortion and homophobic crusades, sometimes accompanied by murders.

They are not even aware of violating Christianity's fundamental principles: love and justice. These Constantinian Christians preach personal conversion and individual piety and philanthropy while having no concern for justice for the most vulnerable populations. For West, these American Constantinian Christians are not aware that their relationship to American political power is of the same order as that of the Christians who signed a pact with the Roman imperial regime. They believe that US imperialism must spread the good borne by the US government. Besides, forgetting who they are, "The corruption of a faith fundamentally based on tolerance and compassion by the strong arm of imperial authoritarianism invested Christianity with an insidious schizophrenia with which it has been battling ever since" (*Democracy Matters*, p. 148).

While many Constantinian Christians are sincere in their faith and actions, they are unaware of their role in the deployment of American imperialism. According to West, these sincere followers are manipulated by Christian leaders and elected imperial officials who have designs contrary to the Christian faith. For him, these sincere Christians must question the vast concentration of power and arrogance of the Constantinian Christian movement's elites. In order to do so, according to West, one can and must revisit prophetic Christianity.

The most progressive social movements in the United States have been led by prophetic Christians: the abolition of slavery, women's suffrage, the development of trade union movements in the nineteenth century, and the civil rights movement in the twentieth century.

> Though the Constantinian Christianity that has gained so much influence today is undermining the fundamental principles of our democracy regarding the proper role of religion in the public life of a democracy, the prophetic strains in American Christianity have done battle with imperialism and social injustice all along and represent the democratic ideal of religion in public life. (*Democracy Matters*, p. 152)

Let us remember that prophetic Christianity is concerned with the poor, the principle of developing public service, and the separation of the state and the Church. In the eyes of West, "The separation of church and state is a pillar for any genuine democratic regime. All non-Christian citizens must have the same rights and liberties under the law as Christian citizens. But religion will always play a fundamental role in the shaping of the culture and politics in a democracy" (*Democracy Matters*, p. 159).

Prophetic Christianity adds a political morality to democracy. Many prophetic Christians were accused of being leftists because they called for people to revolt against the Vietnam War. For West, despite the anathemas launched by Constantinian Christians, the prophetic Christian movement must be vibrant and combative in the age of the American empire. It must above all avoid any compromising adventure with politics.

The Current Affairs of Constantinian Christianity

West sees a direct link between imperial Christianity and the militarily aggressive, authoritarian politics of George Bush's market fundamentalism (*Tragicomique Amérique*, 2005, Préface de Marc Abeles). But according to him, Barack Obama is not exempt and only perpetuates the worst tendencies of neoliberalism and American imperialism. For West, in America, it is Bush who incarnated this Constantinian, imperialist, capitalist American ethos in its hard version, and Obama who embodies it in its soft version. Bush and Obama, in the name of the humanistic values of revealed law, think they have the responsibility to reorganize the world.

Beyond their formal claims of hope of liberation and a better world, these two presidents, alongside Constantinian Christians, participate in

> the glorification of the market [that] has led to a callous corporate-dominated political economy in which business leaders (their wealth and power) are to be worshipped—even despite the recent scandals—and the most powerful corporations are delegated magical powers of salvation rather than relegated to democratic scrutiny concerning both the ethics of their business practices and their treatment workers. (*Democracy Matters*, p. 3)

These standard-bearers of Constantinian Christianity (Bush and Obama) wage war at the international level, reinforce internal inequalities on the one hand, and on the other call for compassion vis-à-vis the poor within and outside of America. According to him, this ambiguity must be denounced and opposed by all those in love with peace and justice, especially when these politicians try to refer to prophetic Christianity in general and to Martin Luther King in particular.

For West, Obama is ill-placed to summon Martin Luther King's thought and approach, while he himself embodies the exact opposite of the approaches, behaviors, and attitudes advocated by King's prophetic Christianity. Prophetic Christianity wants us to be concerned with the most low income in our societies. However, Obama, who quotes King at every turn, is the very picture of these political leaders who put the living conditions of the weakest on the back burner of their political actions. Therefore, Obama cannot claim to embody the values of King.

Moreover, though America is the battleground for religious leaders like King, they have always linked their struggles to those of other peoples. Thus, for King, the massacre of Vietnamese is the very manifestation of American brutality that is exercised *in situ*. This prophetic Christianity allowed King to develop and encourage resistance to injustice regardless of the country (*Hope on a Tightrope: Words and Wisdom*, p. 169). West further asserts that "for all of us who take the cross seriously, the indignation against the cruel treatment of any group of people is an echo of the divine voice" (*Hope on a Tightrope: Words and Wisdom*, p. 169).

For West, prophetic Christianity cannot be considered a mere profession of faith; it is ethics. Any alliance that a religious or political institution seeks to establish with Constantinian Christianity is, according to him, a suicidal process.

Judaism's Dangerous Liaisons with Constantinian Christianity

For West, power games with Constantinian Christians hinder any effort to promote deep democratic identities in the world. This is the case of power games played for geostrategic reasons in the Middle East. For him,

> demagogic and antidemocratic fundamentalisms have gained too much prominence in both Israel and the Islamic world, so too has a fundamentalist strain of Christianity gained far too much power in our political system, and in the hearts and mind of citizens. This Christian fundamentalism is exercising an undue influence over our government policies, both in Middle East crisis and in the domestic sphere, and is violating fundamental principles enshrined in the Constitution; it is also providing support and "cover" for the imperialist aims of empire. (*Democracy Matters*, p. 146)

"What irony," exclaims West, to see an alliance between Jews and evangelical Christians whose present and past anti-Semitism is notorious. He understands that this is "the sense of Jewish desperation during the Yom Kippur War of 1973—fully understandable given the threat of Jewish annihilation only thirty years after the vicious holocaust in Europe—drove the unholy alliance of American Republicans, Christian evangelicals and Jewish neoconservatives" (*Democracy Matters*, p. 165). But he recalls that the support of evangelical Christians is based solely on the idea that the State of Israel paves the way for the second coming of Christ.

For him, these evangelical Christians, who are not concerned with the plight of Jewish and Arab populations, are developing all kinds of strategies to maintain their interests. These evangelical lobbies endorse American power whose shameful and radically undemocratic support for wealthy Arab autocratic regimes that are hostile to the very existence of Israel is well established. By allying with Constantinian Christians, Jewish neoconservatives make a double mistake. On the one hand, they underestimate the imperial designs of America, including against Israel, and on the other, they strip Judaism's universal reach of its humanist content.

According to West, in alliance with the American empire, during the Cold War, these Jewish neoconservatives condemned Israel to assist America in "its dirty work" such as the supply of weapons and support for the Somoza dictatorship in Nicaragua, the Afrikaner apartheid government in South Africa, the National Union for the Total Independence of Angola (UNITA) thugs in Angola, and the juntas of Guatemala. In his eyes, the US government, focused only on its interests, including those of Constantinian Christians, will not hesitate to abandon Israel if need be.

If an oil-rich Arab country could do the dirty work of imperial America better than Israel, cheaply and with less controversy, the United States could very well drop Israel. The history of all imperial powers proves that they do not have friends but rather interests to defend.

Cornel West asks himself the following questions:

> Is there not a long and ugly history of Jews in the Diaspora—Spain, Egypt, Germany—succumbing to false security and assimilationist illusions as they deferred to respective imperial authorities? Is America so different? Do the depths of anti-Semitism in Western Civilization and Christian-dominated societies not reach to the heart of America? What will happen when American imperial elites must choose between oil and Israel? Cannot these elites manipulate anti-Semitic sentiments among the American citizenry the same way they fan and fuel other xenophobic fears for purposes of expediency? (*Democracy Matters*, p. 128)

In answering these questions, West says that there is no doubt that the ties between American empire and the State of Israel have not always been so, and it is likely that they will not always be so. In fact, the current alliance between the United States and Israel did not emerge until the 1960s. Most US political elites supported the Arab states in the 1940s–50s to obtain oil. The first contract for the sale of offensive weapons to Israel was signed in 1965. Israel has certainly become a military giant with nuclear weapons in the Middle East, but this military power and the American protection that comes along with it have not been free. Israel has paid the price: It has neither peace nor real security. The alliance between Constantinian Christians and a branch of Judaism that influences some Israeli governments is based on interests, not convictions.

US–Israel: An Opportunistic Alliance

Constantinian Christians have wanted to make the conflict between Israel and Palestine a religious one when it is, in fact, an internal conflict with imperialism in that "the roots of the conflict go back to the shadows cast by the British empire and the American empire, and now the central presence of American imperial support for the Israeli state as well as the Egyptian and Jordanian states" (*Democracy Matters*, p. 109). He reminds us that the concept of the

> very term "Middle East" was coined in 1902 by a leading American imperialist the U.S. naval officer Alfred Thayer Mahan, to name the geographical space between India and the Arab provinces of the Ottoman empire in an article he wrote about the interests of the Great Powers in the region. In the past, terms such as "Western Asia" or "Turkish Asia" had been used. With the collapse of the Ottoman empire after World War I and the popularizing of the term "Middle East" by the London Times, it caught on, and we seem now to be stuck with it. (*Democracy Matters*, p. 109)

According to West, the imperialist quest for access to oil has left a triple legacy. First, this need to get oil, the real Achilles heel of US foreign policy in the region; then Israel's terrible occupation of Palestinian lands, which violates international law and all codes of humanist ethics; finally, the barbaric suicide bombings that kill innocent people. To this analysis, he adds that "these three fundamental challenges—lack of democracy and presence of anti-Semitic bigotry in oil—rich Arab states, justice for Palestinians, and security for Israel—rest upon promoting deep democratic identities in the region" (*Democracy Matters*, p. 112).

Getting Out of "Constantinianism"

Any resolution of the Israeli-Palestinian conflict must include the struggle against dictatorial Arab regimes, the end of the unjust and ineffective occupation of Palestinian lands, the fight against anti-Semitism, and the recognition of the State of Israel and the rights of the Palestinian people. We must support "Israelis and Arabs who shun bigotry, desire peace, and yearn to be more than pawns in the power games of Israeli, Arab, and American elites.... Within Israel and the Arab world, there are strong traditions to spur this change of the prevailing consciousness" (*Democracy Matters*, p. 112).

For West, we must support and encourage the democratic voices stifled in Arab countries and in Israel (*Tragicomique Amérique*, p. 128). The most conservative elements of the American Jewish elite *accept* the support of conservative evangelical Christians. This alliance between evangelical Christians and conservative Jews "has allowed a downplaying of the suffering of the Palestinian people and a willingness to view the lives of the Palestinians as of less value than these of Jews or Americans.... Prophetic Jews can maintain both the demand for Israeli security and the call for an end to occupation, while also joining with non-Jews who are ready to support them" (*Democracy Matters*, p. 127).

REJECTING RELIGION'S INSTRUMENTALIZATION

For West, the Arab-Israeli conflict is not a religious one, although some would like to pass it off as such. It's a conflict of interests. It is not a conflict between those who are for democracy and those who are against it, for there is a prophetic tradition in which we find the democratic values of tolerance, compassion, and justice in all religious traditions. Indeed, according to West, prophetic witness consists of human acts of justice and goodness that take on human sources of pain and misery. He identifies the causes of unjustified suffering and unnecessary social evils and highlights personal and institutional evils, including being indifferent to these evils:

> The Jewish invention of the prophetic, to be found in the scriptural teachings of Amos, Hosea, Isaiah, Micah, Jeremiah, and Habakkuk, not only put justice at the center of what it means to be chosen as a Jewish people, but also make compassion to human suffering and kindness to the stranger the fundamental features of the most noble human calling. The divine covenant with Abraham, the divine deliverance of enslaved Jews from Egypt, the divine promise of salvation in Isaiah all speak to the core of the prophetic: the distinctive Jewish refusal to allow raw power to silence justice or might to trump right. (*Democracy Matters*, p. 114)

The fundamental question for all peoples is therefore to what extent public interest is focused on the most vulnerable in our society. The Jewish invention of *prophetism* brought this concern to light for the first time.

Judaism: Prophetic Momentum and Political Gravity

West recalls that

> At the heart of the prophetic in the Hebrew scripture is an indictment of those who worship the idol of human power. According to the scripture, since human beings cannot be divine-and often act quite devilishly—prophetic voices must remind Israel of what God requires of them.
>
> To do justice, to love kindness and to walk humbly with your God (Micah 6.8). The very covenant-not contract-between God and Israel is predicated on God's love for justice and Israel's charge: "To keep the way of the Lord by doing righteousness and justice" (Genesis 18:19). The prophetic figures in Israelite history—Jeremiah, Micah, Amos,

Isaiah, and others—give voice to divine compassion and justice in order to awaken human compassion and justice. (*Democracy Matters*, p. 114)

For West, it is sad to see that we go from this ample Judaic vision to the bloodshed, bigotry, myopia, and idolatry that characterize the Israeli-Palestinian conflict! Today, the two peoples have arrogant and stubborn leaders, locked in a growing escalation of violence, who rule above all by manipulating the deep fear and paranoia of their respective peoples—fear and paranoia that are, however, understandable—but, he adds, have been seized by the xenophobes on both sides (*Democracy Matters*, p. 115).

On the one hand, the complicity of Jewish neoconservatives, represented by powerful lobbies and ready to heap scorn on the representatives of prophetic Judaism, is accompanied by the US government's unconditional support to the State of Israel, whose certain policies vis-à-vis Palestinians must be firmly condemned. The Israeli "government refuses to substantially dismantle Israeli's imperial settlements or give up colonial occupation" (*Democracy Matters*, p. 115).

On the other hand, on the Palestinian side, suicide bombers call for the annihilation of the Jews. It is clear that this seemingly dead-end situation cannot be resolved by Palestinians and Israelis alone. The Palestinian government refuses to arrest suicide bombers or punish those who endeavor to push the Jews into the sea. Anti-Arab and anti-Semitic racism limit democratic possibilities for both peoples (*Democracy Matters*, p. 115) West says,

> The barbarity of the terrorism launched against Jews in Israel first by the Arab states and now by the suicide bombers is real and should never be explained away—as the zealots on the Palestinian side do—but the dominant Jewish stance has become so hardened by the pain of this suffering, and by the feeling of being so reviled by enemies, that the Jewish community has been losing touch with its own rich prophetic tradition. (*Democracy Matters*, p. 113)

Similarly, West adds, as Christian elites and some American Jewish factions have settled into a close partnership, critical pacifist voices, including Jewish ones, have been stifled. These Christian elites and Jewish factions have adopted a systematic attitude: "broach no criticisms' position about Israel's actions in the conflict with the Palestinians" (*Democracy Matters*, p. 118).

The prophetic Jewish voices that have condemned Israel's attitude toward the Palestinians have come under tremendous moral and material pressure.

> The experience of Breira is revealing. Breira is Hebrew for "alternative." In the years 1973 to 1977, this group of prophetic American Jews tried to create a democratic space that allowed serious debate about the fate of Israelis and Palestinians beyond the narrow consensus of mainstream American Jewish leadership—a consensus predicated on "ein brera" (there is no alternative to the reigning consensus).
>
> Breira accused the Jewish establishment of a kind of "Israelotry" that blindly worshipped the Israeli state while downplaying Jewish democratic commitments to peace and justice. The group strongly supported the security of Israel and bravely promoted a Palestinian state. Most important, Breira members called for a respectful democratic debate among American Jews regarding the Israeli-Palestinian conflict. And they were viciously attacked and mercilessly crushed—denied membership in local Jewish organizations, forced to quit Breira in order to keep their Hillel rabbi jobs, and cast as self-hating Jews. This antidemocratic response of the mainstream Jewish groups sent chills down the spines of prophetic Jews. For example, the treatment of Rabbi Arthur Waskow was atrocious. His prophetic pro-Israel and pro-Palestine stance was deliberately cast as a terroristic pro-PLO position. He was dubbed a "Jew for Fatah" rather than a concerned rabbi rooted in the rich prophetic tradition of Judaism. Like Rabbi Michael Lerner today, Rabbi Waskow was unfairly labeled a Jewish heretic or traitor. Yet both today persevere against such attacks.

And the present does look more promising. Strong prophetic voices are in fact emerging within the Jewish Diaspora—as well as in Israel—that are putting forward powerful critiques of Israel's handling of the crisis and courageous visions of less violent, more democratic ways forward. (*Democracy Matters*, p. 118-121)

For West, the impressive Jewish civic activism in the United States is aimed at supporting the Israeli government's policies and silencing the prophetic Jews and non-Jews who do not support them. Even if this activism is "far from monolithic and certainly not an almighty cabal of Zionists who rule the United States or the world (in the vicious language of zealous anti-Semites)—[they] are far to the right of most American Jews and are often contemptuous of prophetic Jewish voices" (*Democracy Matters*, p. 11).

In fact, the concern for Israel's security at the expense of the Palestinians' demand for justice not only leads to little security for Israel, but also results in the suffocation of Jewish prophetic heritage. "There are indeed many prophetic Jews eager to pursue honest, Socratic questioning of the hardline position of the US—Israeli alliance, but their voices are marginalized and their motives are often maligned" (*Democracy Matters*, p. 118).

But, fortunately, another part of this community, both in America and in Israel, continues the fight by denouncing the moral hypocrisy of Israel's treatment of Palestinians, with progressive Jews arguing that the prophetic tradition requires a more compassionate, democratic, and just approach (*Tragicomique Amérique*, p. 129). An example is Rabbi Michael Lerner, who, in the footsteps of his master, the great Abraham Joshua Heschel, showed us the way forward (*Tragicomique Amérique*, p. 131). In his book *Healing Israël/Palestine*, Rabbi Lerner writes that

> in the long history of propaganda battles between Zionists and Palestinians, each side has at times told the story to make it seem as if the other side was consistently doing bad things for bad reasons. Both sides have made and continue to make terrible mistakes. As long as each side

clings to its own story, and is unable to acknowledge what is plausible in the story of the other side, peace will remain a distant hope. Those of us who are both pro-Israel and pro-Palestine, who truly believe in the validity of the state of Israel and truly believe in the decency of the vast majority of the Palestinian people, and who will not accept the crude distortions in American media and politics, e.g., that the Palestinians were offered a great deal by Israeli former prime minister Barak, or that the Palestinian people will settle for nothing less than the full destruction of Israel), are systematically excluded when the media represents the sides of the conflict. (*Democracy Matters*, pp. 112–113)

Prophetic Islam—Momentum and Political Gravity

At a time when the world seems to be locked in a growing escalation of "religious" violence, West's analyses of Islam and modernity are extremely relevant. According to him, as with Christianity, there is a nihilist Islam and a prophetic Islam. We must not lump those who carry out terrorist acts to quench their thirst for domination, like the Salafist groups,[11] with the rest of Islam.

These nihilist Islamic groups reject modernity—even as they use it for their propaganda—and consider all those who disagree with their ideologies as "impure." But should we reduce Islam to a religion that is incompatible with modernity as a result? Is this reason enough to declare that this is a war of civilizations between the West and the Muslim world?

Islam's trajectory is inseparable from the world's evolution. We must not think of religions as monolithic and fixed movements. As with all religions, there are ideological currents within Islam.

---

[11] Salafism is a politico-religious movement that claims a return to Islam's origins, based exclusively on the Qur'an and the Sunnah (practices, rules, and immutable laws that come from God). There are several branches of Salafism. Some Salafist groups consider it necessary to proceed by peaceful means (the preachers—predicative Salafism). Others advocate the use of violence to impose Islam as they understand it (the jihadist and takfiri movements).

Likewise, the profound changes brought about by modernity require that religions constantly adapt. Some adapt easily to changes, and others attempt to resist them.

In reality, no religion can survive without borrowing from science, politics, and modern culture. For example, every religion must accept Newton's law of gravity and often has to use contemporary musical instruments in its rituals. The question that must be asked is this: What are the Islamic sources of modernity and the modern sources of Islam? (*Democracy Matters*, p. 132).

Before engaging in an in-depth examination of this question, let's say that for West, if some religious groups are wary of modernity, it is because they believe that imperialist powers are using technology and science to promote their individualistic and materialistic, even hedonistic, culture. In other words, all groups aspire to technology's comforts but are wary of its potentially disruptive effects in social life. Thus, what may appear at a first glance as a rejection of change is only mistrust of a system that uses modernity to institute its imperialist ambitions. Moreover, the turmoil in the contemporary Muslim world is fueled by fears of cultural uprooting and the hopelessness generated by unfettered capitalism.

Muslim populations reject lifestyles and insidious forms of domination and seek to integrate the modern world in terms that preserve their identity (*Democracy Matters*, p. 130). For a very long time, many "Muslim" countries were colonized by Western countries that justified their policies in the name of "civilizing" missions: to bring progress and modernize these countries. At first, peoples (Arab, Asiatic or African) opposed imperial Europe with secular nationalist solutions—solutions that were themselves imitations of insurgent nationalism against empires within Europe itself (Germany in the nineteenth century and Italy against Napoleon) (*Democracy Matters*, p. 136).

Then, those nationalist and secular states presenting themselves as modern states proved to be equally repressive and dictatorial. For example, the military power in Turkey proclaiming itself to be secular and nationalist stands out for the ferocity of its repression of Armenian and Kurdish populations. The same dynamic of repression has taken place in Pakistan, Indonesia, Egypt, and other Muslim countries.

Consequently, a segment of Muslim opinion has perceived these nationalist models as pro-Western and anti-Islamic forms of nationalism that must be eschewed. The questions these people have asked themselves are as follows: What do you do when imperial ideologies and their satellites dehumanize you? How do you build a stable and secure identity and society in the face of the West's onslaught and the internal failures of nationalist regimes?

Some believe they have found solutions by turning to religion. West writes,

> With the collapse of repressive secular nationalism at the top, the Islamic revival mobilized the masses and gained state power. This revival was guided by a particular kind of Islam—a clerical Islam rooted in the religious identity of people and responsive to the pervasive anxieties unleashed by the failure of secular nationalist ideology in the wake of colonial past. (*Democracy Matters*, p. 129)

This is the case with the overthrow of the Iranian Shah's pro-Western regime in 1979 (*Tragicomique Amérique*, p. 152). This revolution was spearheaded by the cleric[12] Ayatollah Khomeini and isn't, according to West, the expression of blind hatred of America: "The quest for an Islamic Identity shuns the uprootedness and restlessness of the modern West and the licentiousness and avariciousness of the American empire. It is similar to any other modern fundamentalist response to certain aspects of modernity" (*Democracy Matters*, pp. 129–130).

---

[12] We cannot properly speak of clerical Islam—as we would do with Judaism or Catholic Christianity—but in certain regions, some Islamic authorities appear to be clergy, especially in Shi'ism. Strictly speaking, Sunni Islam does not have a clergy, but depending on the regions and countries, there are different form of religious authorities: doctors of the law, jurist, head of traditional brotherhood, marabouts, and so on.

Generally speaking, in the face of the failure of secular nationalist experiences, the movements to revitalize Islam—whether fundamentalist or not—appear to be a quest for a new identity. But is this religious identity posture compatible with democratic demands?

"Shiite" or "Sunni" Islamic regimes have applied religious justice based on law that is said to be of divine origin; but in a democracy, the law is an outgrowth of mortals. Should we then draw the conclusion that Islam is incompatible with democracy? Should we exclude this religion from the public sphere? How is Christianity or Judaism more compatible than Islam with democracy?

Let us remember that in all monotheistic religions, there are two branches: nihilistic and prophetic. As we will see in the second part of this book, unlike the nihilistic branch that refuses all criticism, the prophetic branch incorporates criticism in its approach. For West, working for a respectful democracy of religions, and vice versa, is supporting prophetic voices. This is all the more important as the religious traditions will not disappear from one day to the next. These prophetic voices are, *inter alia*, those of Muslim intellectuals who seek to revitalize the rich past of cross-cultural fertilization that has often led Islam to a Socratic examination (*Tragicomique Amérique*, p. 148).

> The path for this critical examination has already been trod by towering Islamic intellectuals—like Fatima Mernissi, Mohamed Abid al-Jabri, Abdokarim Soroush, Mohamed Arkoun, Nawal El Saadawi, Anouar Majid, Tariq Ramadan, Khaled Abou El-Fadl and especially Mahmoud Mohamed Taha—who all question, and examine, the modern West and Islamic traditions in order to forge a new democratic vision in the Muslim world. As Khaled Abou El-Fadl boldly proclaims in his article "Islam and the Challenge of Democracy" in the *Boston Review* (April-May 2003). (*Democracy Matters*, p. 133)

All these authors, each in their own way, have shown how there are interpretative possibilities and tolerant practices in Islamic tradition that are compatible with the democratic system. It is therefore a question of resurfacing those prophetic energies likely to forge a democratic Muslim identity.

> The first step in discerning prophetic energies in Islam and forging an Islamic democratic identity is to put forward a persuasive genealogy of the double developments of Islamic legal thought (Usul al-fiqh and fiqh), theology (Kalam), mysticism (Tasawwuf), and philosophy (falsafa). (*Tragicomique Amérique*, p. 140)

This historical research reveals Isla's broad range of possible interpretations on democratic issues. Not only are there differences with respect to the sources, but also in the interpretations of sharia law. Those who are in favor of sharia reduce the complexities and multiple possibilities of Islam to certain laws and rules. "This is especially so in regard to the crucial question of contemporary Islamic women, since patriarchy is an integral part of Islamic law" (*Democracy Matters*, p. 134).

Depending on the cultures and regions, matrimonial regimes and regulations concerning women differ profoundly. West distinguishes three approaches:

- A first approach starts from legalistic Islamic conceptions of justice itself, *adl* (procedural justice), and *ma'ruf* (positive justice). He shows their compatibility with a democratic conception of justice.
- A second approach to sharia is to undermine the deeply patriarchal character of this Islamic law because Islam is an open way of life.

It is very often the work of women and shows that there are "both pre-legalistic and post-legalistic forms of Islam that sidestep this patriarchal limit in Islam" (Democracy Matters, p. 134).

- Finally, West believes that the third reformist approach can be found in the revolutionary writings of Mahmoud Mohamed Taha (himself murdered by the Nimayri regime in Sudan for his visionary and courageous works). For example, in his manifesto, the *Second Message of Islam*,

  > "Taha conceives of Islam as a holistic way of life that promotes freedom—the overcoming of fear—in order to pursue a loving and wise life. As in the second effort, he and his disciple Abdullahi Ahmed An-Na'im discard the Shari'a and replace it with the Meccan revelation. Taha's conception of good society rests upon economic equality (egalitarian sharing of wealth), political equality (political sharing in decisions), and social equality (no discrimination based on color, faith, race, or sex in order to provide equal opportunity for cultural refinement). (*Democracy Matters*, p. 140)

Long before the rise of clerical Islam, and since the first Islamic State established in 622 by the Prophet Muhammad under the Constitution of Medina, Islam has insisted on mutual respect and civility between Jews and Muslims. The Prophet Muhammad enacted a rule that could be described as constitutional based on an agreement in principle among the Muhajirun (Muslim immigrants from Mecca), the Ansar (the indigenous Muslims of Medina), and the Yahud (the Jews).

West explains that, like all religions, Islam has always incorporated non-religious sources. In fact, the dogmas of Islam that contain non-Islamic sources have

> so routinized and ossified that [they] conceal [their] former contingency and insurgency. In this way, even to be a dogmatic traditionalist is to be part of a dynamic history and ever-changing tradition. This understanding of the fluidity of Islam is required in order for a democratic Islam to challenge the authority of Muslim clerics and Islamic jurists who attempt to naturalize and fossilize their prevailing edicts and decrees. (*Democracy Matters*, p. 135)

Indeed, when one speaks of certain branches of Salafism or the question of "Islamic" veils (Hijab, Chador, Burka, etc.), it is important to emphasize that, depending on the region, there have been borrowings, exchanges, and influences between local cultures and Islam. To better grasp these multiple realities, West invites us to focus on Muslim authors' bodies of literature:

> The paradigmatic literary figures of Samba Diallo in Cheikh Hamidou Kane's inimitable Ambiguous Adventure (1983), Mustafa Sa'eed in Tayeb Salih's powerful Season of Migration to the North (1969), Ken Bugul in Mariétou M'Baye classic the Abandoned Baobab (1991), and Driss Ferdi Chraibi's canonical The Simple Past (1983) all lay bare the inescapable need to confront there islamic tradition. (*Democracy Matters*, p. 131)

All these authors show us Islam in all of its complexity and diversity. In West's eyes, these remarkable writers deserve more attention from those who are interested in Islam, modernity, and democracy:

> In stark contrast to renowned literary figures like Salman Rushdie and V.S. Naipaul, these writers are sympathetic to the Islamic sources of their modern identity and the modern sources of their Islamic identity. These works explore the profound alienation from both sources; and the necessity of building on both sources—all against the West as Imperial agents. (*Democracy Matters*, p. 131)

It is by visiting the works of Muslim thinkers that one can see the sources and conditions of reformulating the dialogue with Islam. "The Islamic quest for a modern identity is situated between Good Friday and Easter, between a past of deep imperial wounds and a forward-looking resurrection" (*Democracy Matters*, p. 132).

As Sheikh Hamidou Kane writes about Western schooling in traditional Muslim Africa,

> The new school shares at the same time the characteristics of cannon and magnet. From the cannon it draws its efficacy as an arm of combat. Better than the cannon, it

makes the conquest permanent. The cannon compels the body, the school bewitches the soul. Where the cannon has made a pit of ashes and of death, in the sticky mold of which men would not have rebounded from the ruins, the new school establishes peace. The morning of rebirth will be a morning of benediction through the appeasing virtue of the new school. From the magnet, the school takes its radiating force. It is bound up with a new order, as a magnetic stone is bound up with a field. The upheaval of the life of man within this new order, is similar to the overturn of certain physical laws in a magnetic field. Men are seen to be composing themselves, conquered, along the lines of invisible forces. Disorder is organized, rebellion is appeased, the mornings of resentment resound with songs of universal thanksgiving. (*Democracy Matters*, p. 131)

In quoting Kane's text, West wants to stress the necessity of dialogue between the West and Islamic countries. For him, the relation between these two parts of the world should neither be a crude clash of civilizations nor an imposition of one upon the other. He states, "Rather it should be a Socratic process of examining a rich past of cultural cross-fertilization" (*Democracy Matters*, p. 132). Just as there is a long Judeo-Christian tradition rooted in prophetic values, there is a long Islamic tradition based on these same values.

It is true that Islam's prophetic dimensions have not often been summarized clearly and aloud by what might be called clerical Islam. Clerical Islam, though geographically delineated, has often opposed "Western universalism" with a "Muslim universalism." The full application of its interpretation of Islam does not represent all of Islam. There are other voices and experiences that have another vision of living together. Those thinkers who deconstruct the internal and external patterns of domination regarding Islam are sometimes misunderstood by Westerners and rejected by Islamists. They denounce the alliances between branches of Islam with political powers in imperialist projects, and they take inspiration from prophecy to experience faith and democracy fully.

These philosophers of Islam face a double challenge: insecurity and political despair. That's why West thinks we have to support them (*Tragicomique Amérique*, p. 148), especially since, for him, the questions they address are the ones we ask ourselves: How do we get out of the cycle of the violence into which the terrorists drag us? Can we heal from the terror in this world?

For West, in order to identify the broad theme of terrorism, we must analyze the sources of evil: capitalism's violence, poverty's breeding ground. Market dogmatism and religious dogmatism intermingle and proceed from the same logic. Their lack of critical rationality devours democratic vitality and leads to nihilism, that is, to the negation of Beings. So, if terrorist groups like ISIS, AQIM, and Boko Haram take advantage of this desperate situation to grow, it is often because certain capitalist powers have forged alliances with them. According to West, listening to progressive Muslims can undermine nihilistic Islamic ideology.

3
VIOLENCE IN AMERICA

In a convergence that cannot be the result of chance, the violence and racism in the US that is currently being reported by the press is a striking corroboration of West's analyses and concerns about the future of democracy in America. He cites the violence that affects political structures, and above all the violence that legitimizes this political violence. This Westian perspective admittedly invites us to perceive violence in America threefold: the real, the imaginary, and the symbolic. His work describes each of these points, and all at once. It addresses the American political and economic system as much in its reality as in its imaginary and its symbolism.

In reality, capitalism's dynamics do not allow a large part of the population to live decently or to have access to the goods and services that the system claims to make available to them, which in turn threatens democracy and living together. Exclusion is inherent in the structures of the American capitalist system.

Certainly, depending on their social positions, people more or less enjoy freedoms, but a good part of the population is excluded. For West, America, which prides itself on being the country of freedom, has a liberticidal political and economic system in reality. To show this, West compares reality to the great national narrative of America: "champion of democracy and freedom." He shows that this self-glorification is linked to the myth of the cowboy and is embodied in symbols that can easily structure beliefs and consciousness.

West reveals the contradictions of the Statue of Liberty, this gift from the French to the US in 1886, located on the tip of Liberty Island. The Statue of Liberty, one of the world's most famous monuments, presents New York and America as the land of freedom in the world and in history. But for him, this symbol, which is America's pride and joy, is at odds with the reality experienced by most people. Certainly, he admits, this frozen statue undeniably has value, a meaning in and of itself, but in reality, it embodies fallacies and illusions when it comes to individual liberties.

For example, according to West, when one takes the Patriot Act or the murder of thousands of innocent people in drone strikes, or the Snowden case, one sees how all these facts and discourse are at odds with the symbols of freedom. This country, which proclaims itself through symbols as the land of freedom, is, according to him, the country of all abuses.

To deconstruct America's discourse, West examines the meaning and effects of the discourse and myths. He shows how these elements insidiously intermingle with and stem from violence. This violence, which spans many registers, needs to be analyzed from several angles: physical, psychological, and sociological, among others. America's violence deeply affects people in their flesh and in their beliefs. It touches sacred values, self-esteem, and social relations. It is a violence knowingly devised by individuals who are interested solely in power and money.

In other words, for West, America was built from violence and has built its identity by oscillating between egocentrism and a so-called universalism. In doing so, it has isolated itself from the rest of the world while believing itself to be the world. This paradox is all the more important as America perceives the world as the object of its desires through the image it creates of itself. By reducing the other to the state of an object, it chooses to neglect them or to consider it according to their interests. This is what West tirelessly denounces under the term *nihilism*: The Other is nothing. In the best-case scenario, the American consciousness perceives the existence of the Other at the margins as a marker of distance.

In this respect, America's distance from other countries can only be measured in terms of competition, conflict, and angst. In the worst-case scenario, the "Other at the margins" does not exist. In any event, for West, the American imaginary as a disposition of intentional consciousness leads to the formation of images of the world that are removed from reality.

Indeed, if the *objet-monde* is present in this imaginary, the real world is absent. America very often adopts a unilateralist or even isolationist stance. It refuses to take criticism from elsewhere and therefore cuts itself off from the rest of the world and the knowledge it could draw from it. This posture only leads to violence and self-destruction. Thus, West writes, "In short, we are experiencing the sad American imperial devouring of American democracy. This historic devouring in our time constitutes an unprecedented *gangsterization* of America—an unbridled grasp at power, wealth, and status" (*Democracy Matters*, p. 8).

He asks the following questions: How do we get out of the infernal cycle of violence? How do we encourage people to build a true democracy? In response, he makes the following statement: "Following the terrorist attacks of September 11, 2001, America has put in place repressive and restrictive measures with respect to rights, such as the Patriot Act."[13]

With respect to this policy of surveillance and punishment that threatens democracy, West believes that an uncompromising analysis of the history of America's terrorism and violence must be conducted. He says that the Bush administration, locked in an isolationist stance, has been deaf to criticism, including that of its allies. The Bush administration adopts the simplistic and aggressive position of "with us or against us." This disdain for the views of others shows how America has dealt with the question of difference. When it comes to defending its interests, America considers itself to

---

[13] The PATRIOT Act can be translated as a law to unite and strengthen the security of America. It is a counterterrorism law that was passed by the US Congress and signed by George W. Bush on October 26, 2001. It allows access to personal files, such as borrowing from libraries; it also allows the FBI to integrate personal data from the private and public sectors.

be the center of the world and is unable to take into consideration the hatred it has sown within and outside its borders for a very long time.

In West's view, the *sine qua non* for resolving these issues is a serious reflection on the sources of evil and an uncompromising analysis of the contradictions of America's political and economic system. This involves questioning the politics of destruction in the conquest and maintenance of power in America. This self-criticism is not meant to invalidate all struggles against any form of internal or external terrorism, but rather to analyze the embedded structures that comprise the discursive component of American politics.

According to West, "The brutal atrocities of white supremacy in the American past and present speak volumes about the harsh limits of our democracy over against our professed democratic ideals" (*Democracy Matters*, p. 14). We cannot understand violence in America today if we do not connect all present situations to past ones. It is not simply about remembering historical tragedies such as the genocide of Native Americans and slavery, but also recalling and showing how this history structures the present condition of Beings. The culture of violence in America is tied to its history.

THE HISTORY AND CULTURE OF VIOLENCE IN AMERICA

West demonstrates that, historically, White supremacists have sought, for example, to remove the truth about the consequences of slavery from America's development process. Supremacists certainly would not want slavery to ultimately define America. But through their segregationist practices, they reproduce the patterns of this horror: gratuitous violence against Black people. This reality that African American populations experience reminds them of periods of segregation and slavery. Certainly, America would like us to forget these periods, but, as Badiou would say, this operation of "subtraction in the field of the nameable" is not possible with the resurgence of racist violence.

In fact, for West, the recent racist violence shows the structuring presence of slavery and the segregationist past. In other words, America's political and social situation is the result of political and economic procedures that are born of slavery. Racist violence against Blacks reminds the world and America of the structural and permanent injustice of the American political and economic system (*Democracy Matters*). Put another way, this horror, even if it is history, is always present because it always makes sense (precisely as nonsense): "We will not ask what the meaning of the event is: the event is the meaning itself."[14]

Even if slavery belongs to a past that can no longer be physically accessed, it remains an eternal evil. Slavery is an eternal truth. Not only does slavery indicate the significance of a drama, but it is also the transfiguration of the present and an opening to the future. The slave system has structured America in the past, it structures it in the present and, if we are not careful, it could reproduce itself here or elsewhere in the future.

We see that what is at stake in the culture and history of violence in America is how the slave event produced what Du Bois calls "color lines," lines and figures of differentiation between Black and White populations. While the history of capitalism is undeniably linked to slavery, this compatibility is developed today in the American prison industry, where prisoners are sometimes treated as slaves.

For West, recalling the history of slavery is not only showing its essence; it's also showing its meaning. To update the role of slavery in the analysis of the political order is also to show how one can move from a reasoning of "essence" to a reasoning of meaning. Broadly speaking, from the analysis he carries out on slavery, West invites us to see how the American capitalist system, structured in economic, political, and cultural subsystems, has the function of organizing Beings as beings for production. He also shows us how there are bridges between the structures of economic production and those of repression.

---

[14] Gilles Deleuze, *Logique du sens* (Paris: Minuit, 1969), 34.

Those excluded from subsystems (economic, political, and cultural) are reintegrated into capitalism's prison system. As we can see, by showing that the issue of slavery is the crux of contradictions in America, West reminds us not only of the need to discuss the "horror" and "catastrophe" of the past, but also invites us to debate structural injustice and violence in the American nation's formation. In fact, according to him, in order to pin down the broad theme of the causes of terrorism, one must ask the following questions: Can one heal from terror in America? How to get out of the cycle of lies and denial into which politicians drag us?

To get out of the violence, it will be necessary to break free of three dominant dogmas that constitute American politics and stifle vital democratic impulses: market fundamentalism, aggressive militarism, and the reinforcement of authoritarianism. These dogmas, which stifle the development and strengthening of democracy in America and the world, are accompanied by three forms of nihilism: evangelical nihilism, paternalistic nihilism and sentimental nihilism.

He adds that

> we are suffering in America today from three particular forms of nihilism, each with its own false justifications and vicious consequences: evangelical nihilism, paternalistic nihilism, and sentimental nihilism. . . . In the true evangelical spirit, such nihilists tend to become militant, broaching no dissenting views. The political nihilism . . . in the form of paternalistic nihilism to be found within the ranks of the Democratic Party, contemporary Grand Inquisitors who long to believe in a grand democratic vision yet cannot manage to speak with full candor or attack the corruptions of the system at their heart. The sentimental nihilists, willing to sidestep or even bludgeon the truth or unpleasant and unpopular facts and stories, in order to provide an emotionally satisfying show. This is the dominance of sentiment over truth telling in order to build up market share. (*Tragicomique Amérique*, p. 27)

For him, it is necessary to lay bare these dogmas and these forms of nihilism to create the conditions for democratic understanding. But "the first step in any criticism of a dogma is to expose its history: to reveal its contingent origins and its humble beginnings" (*Tragicomique Amérique*, p. 28). In the next section, we will see how America develops an aggressive militarism from the myth of the cowboy.

Aggressive Militarism

In West's view, aggressive militarism is based on a policy that ignores the international structures of deliberation. For him, this approach is illegal and immoral: "Like the empires of old—especially the Roman and British ones—what we do abroad affects what we can do here and what we do here shapes what we can do abroad" (*Democracy Matters*, p. 10). According to West, "the American democratic experiment entered the twentieth century as a full-fledged empire with overseas possessions (Hawaii, Cuba, the Philippines, Guam, Puerto Rico, Samoa—attained hegemony over South and Central America" (*Democracy Matters*, p. 31).

He also recalls that the US had militarily intervened in Latin America more than a hundred times in the last 162 years (*Hope on a Tightrope: Words and Wisdom*, p. 179). This imperial policy should be seen in light of the atrocities committed on American soil: the genocide of Native Americans, the terror on Blacks, the enslavement of Africans in America, the crushing of individuals' lives by capitalism's excesses, the mass oppression of minorities, and so forth.

West states that this imperial policy continues today. George Bush and Barack Obama apply the same policy of aggression and bombing. Analyzing Obama's use of drones to indiscriminately bomb entire populations, West says he is the "Global Zimmerman" in reference to the young White man who murdered a young Black man recently in Florida. While West emphasizes the direct responsibilities of the political executive in the killing of innocent people, he also notes their indirect responsibilities. In some cases, he says, American governments delegate this aggressive militarist policy to satellite states.

Hence, in the countries affiliated with the American imperial regime, the populations who are victims of these aggressive policies experience a certain hatred vis-à-vis the West and the United States. Some citizens of these countries end up indiscriminately choosing the path of inadmissible and intolerable terrorism. That said, though these terrorist acts are unjustifiable, so are imperialist policies. And compassionate aid policies will not stop these people who are victims of the injustices of American power. As we will see, for West, these aid policies are part of a paternalistic, sentimental, and evangelical nihilism.

To fight terrorism is to first put an end to Western powers'- aggressive militarist policies, especially the United States. For West, as long as the US state refuses to change its international policy, we cannot cure terrorism. Within and without, aggressive militarism and authoritarianism are justified by the policy of retaliation or the prevention of terrorism.

Authoritarianism

According to West, the September 11, 2001, attacks were a blessing for strengthening all controls. We settled into a sort of paranoia that sees potential terrorists everywhere and induces the loss of the very values of dialogue, communication, and respect for others that are supposed to be the cornerstones of democracy (*Tragicomique Amérique*, p. 27). Authoritarianism leads to the indiscriminate indictment of honest citizens. It extends to the police power that feeds the prison industrial complex and legitimizes violence and the abuse of power.

He notes that the United States has the world's largest relative number of prisoners. It is also the country with the highest number of prisoners on the basis of ethnicity. In 2010, 46 percent of long-term inmates were Black, who represent approximately 12 percent of the US population. Likewise, one out of every ten African Americans in their thirties is in prison, is going to go to prison, or has been in prison[15] once in their lifetime. Based on a federal law on drug penalties (crack/cocaine), we are targeting the low income. Proportionally, it is among Blacks that the poverty rate is highest. This leads to racial discrimination against African Americans, who comprise the largest group (84.7 percent) of people convicted for the possession of crack, which is called the drug of the poor, whereas they represent only 27 percent of people convicted of cocaine possession.

But this policy that targets minorities is only enriching capitalists because, with the financial crisis, poverty is on the rise. So, the more low income people there are, the more prisoners there are, and the higher the share prices of the prison industry are on the stock market. This industry is growing all the faster as its privatization continues to expand. For West, what can be understood and contemplated through the "prison industry" is the inhumanity of the American capitalist system and the humanity of imprisoned beings.

Certainly, we cannot legitimize the use of drugs that leads people to destroy themselves, but we must understand why despair causes so many Blacks down this path of destruction. Yet, what interests the elites is not the humanity of Beings but their being, that is, their economic or political utility.

Market Fundamentalism

Market fundamentalism consists of pretending that all the systems of production and consumption must depend on the law of supply and demand. All mechanisms of regulation or alignment and

---

[15] Since the mid-1980s, the narcotics penalty laws have established a disparity of one to one hundred for crack and cocaine: A person with five grams of crack is given the same sentence (five years under federal law) as a person with five hundred grams of cocaine. We know that crack is consumed by the low income. According to the *Observatoire des Inégalités*, November 17, 2011, between 2000 and 2010, in the United States the number of those who are low income rose from 31.6 to 46.2 million, and the poverty rate from 11.3 to 15.1 percent.

determination of prices and quantities of products or services are made on the basis of the market. But, across markets, despite the claim of exercising freedoms, we note the existence of an exclusionary logic of "those without capital." West pushes us to reflect on the link between market and democracy. How can the market guarantee social justice and play an active role in the exercise of freedoms, including freedom of enterprise? How do you reconcile the demands of democracy and those of the market? In principle, the market and democracy allow for a complex combination of freedoms and social justice. But the market and democracy are never strangers to the stakes of life, the urgencies of everyday life, the misfortunes and happiness of Beings.

In order for the market to appear as a democratic place, not only will it have to allow for legal equality among people, and for the autonomy and freedom of everyone, but also for it to be subject to control by people. For the market and democracy to work, the institutions that are supposed to represent them must also be invested, credible, and loved in their symbols. Normally, any delegation of power by the community must belong to all citizens and the institutions that represent it.

However, through market fundamentalism West shows that it is the richest who benefit from monopolies and control the production and distribution circuits. By transferring a part of the people's sovereignty to a class of "plutocrats," the rulers do not allow democracy to function fully. For West, the plutocrats who maintain the economic order by relying on a coercive order cannot be trusted.

The test of the market is a test of political power's violence. The market's utilitarian logic seems to reject the utopia of a universal ethic based on critical reasoning. It is this lack of rationality specific to dogmatism that devours democratic vitality, which also leads to nihilism. West says we are currently witnessing "an unprecedented gangsterization of America—an unbridled grasp at power, wealth, and status" (*Democracy Matters*, p. 8). The same is true of the authoritarianism and religious militarism based on the myth of the cowboy, and of market fundamentalism as a dramatic revival of a certain Constantinian religious fundamentalism.[16]

In fact, the model of the cowboy shows that for the United States, military power represents salvation in a world where whoever possesses the most powerful weapons is the most moral and virile, and therefore the worthiest of policing others (*Tragicomique Amérique*, p. 26):

> free market fundamentalism—just as dangerous as the religious fundamentalisms of our day—trivializes the concern for public interest. The overwhelming power and influence of plutocrats and oligarchs in the economy put fear and insecurity in the hearts of anxiety-ridden workers and render money-driven, poll-obsessed elected officials deferential to corporate goals of profit, often as the cost of common good. This illicit marriage of corporate and political elites—so blatant and flagrant in our time—not only undermines the trust of informed citizens in those who rule over them. It also promotes the pervasive sleepwalking of the populace, who see that the false prophets are handsomely rewarded with money, status, and access to more power. (Democracy Matters, p. 4)

Therefore, to reflect upon market fundamentalism in America is to reflect upon American capitalism's singularity: its ethics. For West, what emerges in the context of the new "Bush" impulse of market fundamentalism in America is the inauguration of practices and mechanisms of economic violence that break the vital continuity of social systems of solidarity; it is a challenge to democratic life. In addition to market fundamentalism, authoritarianism, and aggressive militarism, democracy in America today suffers from nihilism.

---

[16] As explained in the preface, West uses the term "Constantinian Christianity" to identify a form of Christianity that is complicit with power. It is in reference to the Roman emperor who, in the fourth century, legalized Christianity and chose to rely on the Church to bolster his power.

NIHILISM IN AMERICA

> In our postmodern world of pervasive consumerism and hedonism, narcissism and cynicism, skepticism and nihilism, the Socratic love of wisdom and prophetic love of justice may appear hopeless. *Cornel West*

For West, what is seen today in America's political and economic system is the inhumanity in the behavior and actions of political elites. This system, apart from its instruments of domination (army, police, economic and financial institutions), builds institutional and psychological barriers through "a market morality devoid of all faith in the liberation of people or in the hope of freedom" (*Tragicomique Amérique*, p. 25); it gives no chance to the low income and prevents the democratic process. In West's eyes, nihilism is slowly killing democracy in America. It is a pernicious and dangerous attitude, because it hinders democracy's development.

It is pernicious because it is based on the ideology that the individual who cannot make the most of the American system and does not share the capitalist vision of the world is a non-being. In other words, every normal being must cherish the American political and economic system. Any citizen whose voice is dissonant with the "values" of the American system hardly deserves the status of a full citizen. This view of the Other makes the authentic links disappear. Similarly, at the international level, states that cannot follow America's suit are unworthy states. Therefore, by force or by will, the American vision must be imposed everywhere.

> This American political system finds its foundation in a complex mixture of democratic commitment and nihilist imperialism. In fact, America entered the twentieth century with domestic racist systems of terror over Black, Brown, Asian and Native peoples. It also had attained hemispheric hegemony ... by giving new force and enforcement to the Monroe Doctrine, which in 1823 first stipulated US imperial "sovereignty" over the South American and Central American nations. (*Democracy Matters*, p. 32)

He adds this:

> The most frightening feature of imperial America is neither the myopic mendaciousness of the Republican Party nor the paternalistic spinelessness of the Democratic Party (though the Democratic spine has been stiffening in response to the egregious excesses of Bush). Instead, what is most terrifying—including the perennial threat of cowardly terrorists—is the insidious growth of deadening nihilisms across political lines, nihilisms that have been suffocating the deep democratic experiences. (*Democracy Matters*, p. 26)

Nihilism is therefore only graspable and comprehensible if we take into account the organic ties between politics, the economy, myths and religion, on the one hand, and on the other, vested interests at the national and international levels.

These nihilists are found among some national and international religious, media, and political elites. They make and break institutions according to their interests. They are responsible for the decline of democracy in America, and they stifle its development in the rest of the world.

According to West, in America, these elites incarnate three forms of nihilism, respectively: evangelical nihilism, sentimental nihilism, and paternalistic nihilism. But this classification does not exclude shifts, agreements, and flows among these people.

Paternalistic nihilism consists of being a protector of democracy, whereas the sentimental nihilist is incapable of speaking sincerely or of attacking the heart of the corruption of the system that infantilizes citizens. Paternalistic nihilists believe that they are the guarantors of the well-being of the people and that the latter owes them, in return, respect and obedience. In doing so, they infantilize the people by trying to maintain a relationship of dependence, of subordination, that hides the capacity for analysis.

For West, paternalistic nihilism is the prerogative of both parties. Though it was Bush who represented paternalistic and evangelical nihilism in the recent past, Obama represents the figure of paternalistic and sentimental nihilism today. Obama participates cynically in abuses of power, as the Grand Inquisitor[17] of Dostoyevsky's *Brothers Karamazov* might say.

Sentimental nihilism is also too present in the media: Instead of acting to change the living conditions of people, there is a tendency to be moved by their fate. According to West, this nihilism uses different stratagems to gain market share and devitalizes the reality that is lived by the people. It is the work of the megaphones that are more interested in their individual advantages than in the smooth running of society.

As for evangelical nihilism, it refuses all contradictions and blocks all contestation in the name of a truth supposedly drawn from the gospel. It is the hawks of the Bush administration who most closely incarnate this evangelical nihilism and who are

> drunk with power and driven by grand delusions of American domination of the world. And they have been willing to lie and to abuse their control of American power in order to pursue that dominance. Unlike their idol, Ronald Reagan—a masterful conservative communicator and true believer in the rightness of America's might—the new hawks seem to believe that America might actually determine what is right. In this tradition of thinking, we wouldn't be so powerful if we weren't right, so our might shows that we are right. Accordingly, America's power justifies the refusal to listen to or reply to our critics, be they former allies in the United Nations or fellow citizens of goodwill demonstrating in the streets. America's hubris means only that our power moves must be forms of empowerment for others. What we do must be a force for good for others, even if others disagree, dissent, or even are harmed. President Bush and his inner circle have acted like exemplary evangelical nihilists—present-day

---

[17] The disenchanted priest who cynically participates in abuses of power yet recognizes the capacity for perversion of true faith.

Thrasymachuses—who show no respect for Socratic questioning of their positions and actions. They even characterize such questioning as unpatriotic. (*Democracy Matters*, p. 31)

Thus, though evangelical nihilism is the prerogative of Constantinian Christians, it is none the less true that the Republican Party, eager for imperialism and the benefits of the market, uses it. Similarly, while sentimental nihilism is conveyed by the media in general, the Democratic Party also uses it to satisfy its ends.

How do we live together if relations are based on the exclusion of a large part of the people? How can America claim to be grounded in the rule of law when it favors nihilism, which is a form of violence? Does the logic of violence not lead to the negation of substantial realities such as the existence of others?

Nihilism is based on so-called values and dogmas. It is in the name of the values of public safety, the market, and religion that human lives are crushed. The rational core of all these dogmas being market fundamentalism, it is therefore necessary to demystify and demythologize it, particularly showing its characteristics and its effects in social life.

> The dogma of free market fundamentalism has run amok, and the pursuit of profits by any legal (or illegal) means—with little or no public accountability—guides the behavior of the most powerful and influential institutions in our lives: transnational corporations. (*Democracy Matters*, p. 47)

The dogma of market fundamentalism can only lead to forgetting or denying the Being. In other words, market dogma leads to political nihilism because nihilists consider it necessary to let the laws of the market take their course—any voluntarist approach is senseless or even harmful. In this way, with economic and political nihilism, we are witnessing a negation of the Being's significance.

This market-based system is set up by political leaders and plutocrats who want to maintain the capitalist order for their own interests. These immoral nihilists who seek to maintain the system of capitalist domination in the United States and in the world control most material and intellectual production apparatus. West writes, "These pervasive nihilisms in American democracy today have made way for a resurgent imperialism—the ultimate expression of the market-driven grasp for power. The nihilistic market-dominated mentality—the quest for wealth and power—leads to the drive for conquest" (*Democracy Matters*, p. 39).

In other words, these nihilists are ready for anything to satisfy their hunger for domination. They do this through the promotion of market fundamentalism, aggressive militarism, and authoritarianism within and outside of America. West shows that these policies accompanied by a so-called religious morality serve to hide the capitalist system's emotional, existential, ethical, reactive, and violent issues. The blind application of market laws does not only objectify Beings and individuals. It erodes the systems of the possibilities for a collective life such as democracy.

With their arrogant attitudes and their feelings of superiority, these plutocrats and their political allies put in place devices of alienation. This deliberate strategy of the politico-economic elite is particularly aimed at neutralizing the poor. Alienation is reflected in the latter by a self-destructive debauchery, an unbridled taste for materialism, consumption, and the objectification of women and sex.

Very often, when they do not turn to terrorism, individuals who fail to keep pace with this ultra-consumerist society commit suicide physically or psychologically and/or spiritually through the excessive use of drugs and alcohol.

Those who resist generally dispose of community self-defense resources and institutions. These attitudes of community defense are treated as communitarianism. Of course, it is a retreat, but instead of going into deviance or mistrust, people are trying to cope by using the social, economic, and cultural resources that their communities can provide.

But these nihilists seek by all means to weaken those who resist them. Low-income people are accused of marginalizing themselves. But the attitudes of withdrawal of populations generally derive from the consequences of ultraliberal policies. By removing the minimum necessary for the low income to ensure their daily lives, we end up infusing these policies of exclusion into the heads of some minority leaders. These policies, similar to the racial separation laws put in place by Jim Crow and White supremacists, are thus sometimes replicated and reproduced by leaders of certain racial minorities.

These ultraliberal economic strategies that deny the social realities experienced by minorities are developed by plutocrats at the service of the Republican and Democrat Parties. All ignore or discredit the structural and historical problems of communities. These ideological prescriptions are also taken up by many leaders of minority groups. The latter justify them and are sometimes zealous for their application in their communities. Is everything ensnared?

White Supremacy's Social Reproduction of Nihilism in the Black Community

West does not only criticize the nihilism produced by White supremacists; he also criticizes the Black community. The nihilism of White and ultraliberal supremacy is reproduced in other minority groups. This is the case of a certain Black bourgeoisie that sustains the same process in the African American population.

According to West, on the one hand, the increasing nihilism in Black America is the "lived experience of coping with a life of horrifying meaninglessness, hopelessness, and (more important) *lovelessness*" (*Democracy Matters*, p. 26). On the other hand, it is the effects of the racial question and Black leadership in the United States that lead to the alteration of the links. According to West, these Black leaders, who are too hungry to be angry, too impatient to be bold, too self-invested to be provocative, are not only dangerous to their community, but the entire American nation (*Democracy Matters*, p. 27).

In favor of their own interests, these types of Black leaders are capable of espousing ideologies that are harmful to social harmony. In this logic, some Black leaders will deny the existence of racial problems in the United States in order to curry favor with their White peers, and vice versa. Moreover, in order to justify their policies and maintain the social structures of domination and social reproduction, Whites who dominate the political scene seek to nominate the least competent Blacks to positions of responsibility, saying "There, we appoint them to responsibilities, but they are not capable." Similarly, to avoid being criticized by their own, no Black leader dares to denounce the appointment of an incompetent Black to a position of responsibility.

The nihilism of White normative culture thus affects the history, context, and culture of Americans of African descent. In analyzing this phenomenon, West proposes a typology of African American leadership. For him, there are three types of Black leaders:

- *Leaders who want to erase their racial identity.* They seek to be seen as people for whom the racial question does not exist. Feeling uncomfortable about the way their White middle-class peers look at them, and eager to gain respectability, some go so far as to speak out against government-sponsored initiatives like affirmative action, when it is precisely to this type of program that they owe their "success."
  This nihilism is carried by an elite less devoted to their community than to their own interests. These Black leaders who agree to play the rules of the game set by White America are often able to obtain high positions. These leaders very often defend their personal interests and refuse to tell the truth.
- *Protesters who claim their racial identity.* They only identify with the Black race and use it as a broker before other races. In fact, the feeling of otherness is so entrenched in their minds that it is difficult for them to reconcile African American culture with White American normative culture despite the links between these two cultures. They let themselves be trapped in the ethnocentric imagination. Ethnocentrism is a belief that focuses systematically and exclusively on a particular group and does not allow for the consideration, even theoretically, of measures that can bring the greatest benefit to others if it does not belong to the group.
- *The prophetic leaders who acknowledge racial problems but try to have a more global vision.* These prophetic leaders who refuse and reject the destructive strategy of ultraliberalism are stigmatized. They are referred to as people who refuse to integrate.

For West, "it is the profoundly democratic, prophetic Christianity of Martin Luther King Jr. that is the source of inspiration for these leaders. Indeed, all the great Black political leaders are a product of the Black religious tradition. From slave and preacher Nat Turner to Reverend King, from Frederick Douglas to Pastor Clayton Powell, from Marcus Garvey to Malcom X, or from Booker T. Washington to Reverend Jesse Jackson, the fusion of religion and politics is strikingly evident. And, in most cases, the religious background is Christian" (*Tragicomique Amérique*, p. 84).

For West, it is this Christianity marked by strong prophetic tendencies that allowed part of the Black community to confront and survive slavery and allowed preachers to organize slave revolts in the nineteenth century. The commitments of these men strongly illustrate the crucial role of the Black Church in the fight for the liberation of Black Americans. West adds that, today, it is this Christianity that constitutes the main source from which Blacks can draw strength and comfort when confronted with the capitalist order of modern America (*Cornel West*, Le rôle prophétique des Églises, *le Monde Diplomatique*, November 1983).

But, he notes, some who claim to embody the values of King refuse to make the condition of the weakest the heart of their political action. According to him, they must be unmasked.

Barack Obama's Nihilism and Religious Prophecy

In his eyes, Obama, who quotes King at every turn, is the very figure of this category of gravediggers. For him, Obama not only seeks to erase his racial identity to better sneak into the White world, but refuses to work for the universal good that is the heart of Dr. King's struggle. Obama, whom some have called "post-racial," is part of the leaders who are quick to erase their racial identity to better satisfy their personal designs. For West, this type of leader who has a strong feeling of insecurity is a threat to freedom because he reinforces a certain fear of the free Black man, and whoever is afraid of the Black man's freedom is afraid of the freedom of the Being. Thus, the American president's consideration for the rich and powerful is a sign of uncertainty, a lack of confidence, in dealing with racial and economic inequalities. He surrounds himself with men and women close to the plutocrats who are more interested in US imperialist and capitalist domination than in democracy and social justice.

In short, for West, Obama is not a brave man: "I think my dear brother Barack Obama has a certain fear of free black men," West said. "It's understandable. As a young brother who grows up in a white context, brilliant African father, he's always had to fear being a white man with black skin. All he has known culturally is white. ... When he meets an independent black brother, it is frightening. Obama, coming out of Kansas influence, white, loving grandparents, coming out of Hawaii and Indonesia, when he meets these independent black folks who have a history of slavery, Jim Crow, Jane Crow and so on, he is very apprehensive," West said. "He has a certain rootlessness, a deracination. It is understandable."

West continues:

> I was under the impression that he might bring in the voices of brother Joseph Stiglitz and brother Paul Krugman. I figured, given the structure of constraints of the capitalist democratic procedure that's probably the best he could do. But at least he would have some voices concerned about working people, dealing with issues of jobs and downsizing and banks, some semblance of democratic accountability for Wall Street oligarchs and corporate plutocrats who are just running amuck. I was completely wrong.

West feels a strong sense of disappointment with Barack Obama. But, beyond the sentimental aspects that may appear in this scathing criticism, we have seen that there is a difference in the interpretation of King's legacy. To understand this issue, let's take a closer look at the interpretation of King's legacy through, on the one hand, Obama's *Audacity of Hope* and on the other, West's *Hope on a Tightrope*. As we immediately notice, these two books deal with hope.

For both, this hope-based title implies the idea of conviction, belief, hope, and expectation of something that can change a negative or painful situation. Each one of them shows that he always hopes for the arrival of a situation, a movement in the direction of individual and/or collective interest. But hope remains uncertain and mysterious; even if we base it on an intimate perception, nothing guarantees its realization. For Obama, we must have the audacity to hope despite the difficulties, while, for West, certainly we must hope, but the social, economic, and political environment shows that this hope is on a tightrope.

In exchange for *Audacity of Hope*, which, according to West, favors compromise and negotiations with the "establishment plutocrats," West proposes *Hope on a Tightrope*, which favors risk, prophecy, rebel thinking. For Obama, hope is a kind of optimism based on the probable, whereas in West it is based on indeterminacy and faith. There is a fundamental breaking point between two visions, religious and pragmatist.

Obama thinks that, in the public domain, one must relativize faith's possibility to transcend concerns; pragmatism must prevail over prophecy. Thus, in 2006, while he was a senator, he said, "Democracy demands that the religiously motivated translate their concerns into universal rather than religion-specific values. It requires their proposals to be subject to argument and amenable to reason."[18] For West, while democratic debate requires that reason be included, it also requires consideration of all points of view, including religious ones.

To end the debate temporarily, let us say that Obama and West are strongly marked by religion. But while the latter clearly assumes his attachment to the Baptist Church, the former does not clearly show his belonging to the same Church. The strong

---

[18] From Senator Barack Obama's 2006 keynote address at the Call to Renewal's Building a Covenant for a New America conference in Washington, D.C. The event was sponsored by evangelical activist Jim Wallis and *Sojourners*.

education he has received from his maternal side certainly plays into his hesitations. Our hypothesis is that Obama is torn between the Baptist Church and other Protestant churches.

Belonging to a given church, Evangelical, Baptist or Methodist, indeed implies a different conception of the articulation between the political and the religious. For example, the Baptist places more emphasis on group life, solidarity, while the Evangelical emphasizes individual autonomy and strong institutions.

If, for Obama, ideals without power do not amount to much, for West, power without ideals can only lead to nihilistic self-perpetuation. But for West, ideals do not boil down to just religion. He therefore makes a clear case for the clear-cut separation between religion and politics, even though religion can serve as a source of inspiration for politics. In fact, for him, in a country where 80 percent of the population call themselves Christians (mainly Constantinian), 72 percent of whom say they are waiting for Christ's second coming, and 40 percent say that they speak intimately to God at least twice a week, "the battle for the soul of American democracy is, in large part, a battle for the soul of American Christianity, because the dominant forms of Christian fundamentalism are a threat to the tolerance and openness necessary for sustaining any democracy" (*Democracy Matters*, p. 146). West doesn't see any contradiction between true democratic leadership and true Christianity. He thus refuses to withdraw from the politico-religious space, saying he speaks as a Christian whose commitment to democracy is very deep, but whose Christian convictions are even deeper. It is this influence of religious prophecy, pragmatism, and the blues in West's commitment that we will see in the next chapter.

4
FROM REVOLT TO THE ELABORATION OF REBELLIOUS THOUGHT

Throughout part one of this book on the sources of engagement, we see that the young West addresses the collisions between religion and politics and violence and nihilism in America with both personal experiences and America's collective history. For this philosopher and believer, the various American governments have always effectuated complex mixtures of democracy and nihilist imperialism. They have justified their imperial aggression in the name of democratic values. The plutocrats subject their nation's institutions to their pecuniary interests. The political parties, be they Democrat or Republican, apply policies of exclusion and violence. All of them pervert democratic gains and human relations.

Remember, the questions that are at the heart of West's general problematic are the following: How do you inscribe the nonexistent? Where does the discord come from in American society? What are the vanishing points of the political system?

He observes that arrogance, imperialism, the ideology and postures of exceptionalism, and America's aggressive behavior can only destroy peace and democracy. He shows, for example, that the PATRIOT Act, the US government's opinion monitoring system, does not simply disrupt freedom, it also undermines the foundations of living together: critical rationality, compassion, and hope (*Tragicomique Amérique*, p. 7). In other words, the PATRIOT Act is the weakening of the conditions of understanding, democracy, and the dehumanization of human beings.

Tracing the PATRIOT Act's forms of oppression, West shows that it is spreading throughout the world in the defense of imperialism. Thus, if American soil is fertile ground for analyzing violence and injustice, we must extend the analysis wherever rabid capitalism unfolds. In short, West's questions extend beyond his country's borders. In different parts of the world, some might ask, how can a country that has built and continues to build its power and economy on the basis of violence claim to embody democracy? How do we get out of the infernal cycle of violence? How do we encourage people to build a true democracy?

Though, on the surface, one can feel the devastating radiation of racism, West shows that the ideology that incubates this incredible violence is not extinguished. It is submerged in the bowels of the ultraliberal economy. He therefore proposes a philosophy of the social contract based on historical and sociological African American thought that could, under certain conditions, be extended elsewhere.

This search drives West to reflect on the religious prophecy and Afro-American music. Inspired by these thoughts, he believes that humanity will find ways, means, and conditions to live together.

PART TWO

Poetics, Philosophy and Ethics of Engagement

In the eyes of West, America is witnessing a kind of abandonment of all democratic ideals. Many political and intellectual actors think that the great ideals of peace, justice, and coexistence are obsolete, and for them, what is important is individual success by whatever means possible. Democracy is entrusted to individuals and institutions that are preoccupied with their personal interests above all else.

But to live together, we need a democracy driven by virtuous people because it is the system that is supposed to allow citizens to participate effectively in societal life and in the life of the nation. Critical reasoning is what shapes reality and democracy's core as a link and as a potency. The power of critical reasoning is that it critiques itself. It allows democracy to empower freedom.

Indeed, the logic of democracy is the expression of freedoms and liberties, of getting people to speak, of iterating citizens' convictions in a rational, credible, and viable framework. West notes that American citizens have neither the same tools nor the same economic, cultural, and social capital to have equal access to institutions and markets. It is therefore necessary to reform and improve the institutions that are charged with embodying democracy. To do this, the intellectual has a duty to engage.

Thus, posing as democracy's shield, West denounces the false postures of the elite. He participates in and is arrested at political protests. This university intellectual elite hailing from "visible/invisible" minorities allows himself to be caught up in this dialectic in order to then attempt to transcend it. This approach, as we will see, is not without risk. Through his positions and his commitment to the outcast, West takes the risk of being loved by some and hated by others. In fact, he is aware that really engaging in group action for a just cause can lead to misunderstandings or suspicions on the part of opponents. This risk is all the greater in American society when one is allied with the marginalized, the "voiceless," the low income, the outcasts.

For West, the intellectual's mission is to bring democracy into play everywhere. Citizens must become involved in the life of the nation. As for the state, it must always take into account the demands of citizens, especially the weakest. He believes that American society, particularly the culture of the marginalized populations, offers resources to reinvigorate social bonds and living together. Inspired, for example, by religious prophecy and the blues, he believes that the nation can find the resources necessary for a democratic and harmonious life. These marginalized spaces are also sites where thought can be renewed. We will first see how he uses the blues to reflect on democracy and justice. Then we will show how he uses religious prophecy and pragmatism to elaborate his thought. Finally, we will show how blues and jazz allow him to develop his concept of prophetic pragmatism and to gain an ethic of commitment.

5

BLUES THINKING

I am a bluesman in the life of the mind, and a jazzman in the world of ideas.

Cornel West (Brother West: Living and Loving out Loud)

It is one of the great lessons I learned from surrealism: it is the conception of poetry not as an effusion but as a means of detection, as a means of revelation. Poetry as access to the Being, as access to oneself, and of course for me, access to deep forces; it is the geyser and it is the eruption, the eruption of these forces so long buried and obscured by debris and slag.

Aimé Césaire[19]

Like Césaire's quote about poetry, with West, blues and jazz are modes of access to the Being. They help to detect, to reveal, what is hidden in oneself and in the Other. This African American music also expresses thoughts about life's movements and demands, about freedom, and they provide tools to reflect on the individual and collective future. By giving these forms of Afro-American music[20]

---

[19] Daniel Maximin, *Aimé Césaire, Frère Volcan* (Paris: Seuil, 2013), 223.
[20] The time of music is not only a poetic time or a political time, it is also a political and poetic space where Black Americans can still build the consciousness of themselves in the obscurity of subjective trajectories as a people whose humanity has been denied.

the status of thought, West shows how they activate hidden truths and point to other opportunities for social harmony.

Blues is a force of remembrance and of hope. It is a method that founds another type of legitimacy through an overture of speech: dialogue. The blues is also "rebel" thinking that transgresses all lines and borders and calls for the establishment of a combatant solidarity chain among all those concerned with equality and justice. The crux of this thinking is to reveal the presence of the "forgotten," to confer the status of being on the nonexistent. Blues allows the Black individual to pass, to slip from nonexistence to being, and from the non-being (the Black individual devoid of all humanity) to existence (the Black maestro of music). The bluesman associates virtually everyone with his thinking and his conclusions and beckons the decision to change the world.

Shifting with the perspective of the blues, and all African American music in general, West gives us an analytical framework to understand America's contradictions from within on the one hand, and to provide elements to reflect on the universal on the other hand. By leading us into marginalized spaces, African American artists, especially bluesmen, allow us to grasp the differences in temporality: the time of the excluded, the time of the elites. The artistic practices of these populations constitute an object of research for philosophers. But does this Westian analysis of the blues concern the rest of the world?

Blues expresses pain and brings joy. It opens up a universal utopia (a better world for all). It suggests an ideal of a world without outcasts. This ideal that motivates the outcasts' struggle against despair and despondency can create enormous opportunities for all the wretched peoples of the earth who do not pass on exploring all peaceful solutions. The blues ethic is rooted in the feeling of universal compassion that corresponds to humanism.

For West, the blues is a concept, a normative idea, a feeling. This theoretical sketch of African American art allows him to produce a philosophy of multiplicity versus unity and a philosophy of a fragmented world unity at the same time. In short, this art, which universalizes African Americans' singular experience, makes it possible, at the same time, to reach Beings' truths and to find new bases to reorganize their world and the world. It is therefore a way of thinking that invites sharing.

Broadly speaking, West shows that through the blues, African Americans have a dual identification: identification in music as representation and identification in the social realm to rebuild social bonds from a standpoint of nonexistence. This twofold identification is expressed through the articulation of three types of social relations: external relations (musical form), breath relations (the narrative, collective novel), and the relations of representations (lifestyles).

These are the modes of identification and articulation found in all Afro-American music. The significance of African American artists' attitudes can be seen as much on the axiological level (appreciation, evaluation) and on the praxis level (gesture, posture) as on the cognitive level (knowledge, perception). This triple possibility of reception, judgment, and knowledge renders this African American art thought.

By using blues thinking, one can go beyond one's perceptions and hear the productions of others' thoughts to understand the essential place of the Being. This music invites all those concerned with equality and justice to set up a combatant solidarity chain. Blues and jazz bring together the different populations, get them to dialogue, connect them, and detach them from the cycle of violence.

Indeed, the bluesman and the jazzman play on variations of themes and melodies that capture society's nuances, borders, and fragments. They pave the path to encounters. In the forms borrowed by blues and jazz, each voice, in its singularity and exceptionality, feeds the orchestra, the group, the collective.

Similarly, the African American artist, whether it is a rapper, bluesman or jazzman, invites us to see how we slip from nonexistence to life. This means that artists can play the role of intermediary in the identity movements between the Being and the non-being, existence and nonexistence, integration and exclusion, and so on.

Ignoring this thinking is also letting an important source of essential praxis get away from African American populations. As Roland Barthes would say, in the bluesman's musical production, "there is the general choice of a tone, an ethos, ... where [he] shows himself clearly as an individual because this is where he commits himself."[21]

REBEL THOUGHT

Blues and jazz, which have played a major role in African American resistance movements and in America's cultural formation, not only trace the history of Black populations, but also show ways to build a harmonious society. Their melodies not only bridge the disjunction between White American culture and African American culture, they also allow for grasping the disparities between rich and poor, educated and uneducated, and so on. They have a spiritual dimension since they encourage us to forget our material and social conditions to forge ahead.

If the blues forges resilience and brings hope, jazz pulls the audience and the musician upward through improvisation and with innovation. West writes that "while supremacists' absolutist and rigid mentalities lead to spiritual impasses, with his improvisations the Jazzman helps us to keep the world in a fluid and flexible perspective" *(Brother West: Living and Loving out Loud,* p. 173).

In jazz and blues, not only individual feelings are expressed, but so is the way the group favors the subjects' dramatic value. These forms of music reveal truths enveloped in various social and cultural experiences. By allowing individuals to express their freedom, jazz contributes to democratic expression. Indeed, each jazz musician must listen to the other's solo and then take over to speak in turn.

As for the blues and rap, they are breaches used by the outcast to light a fire that blows up certainties. According to West, all the Afro-American music that amazes everyone, including the racists themselves, only offers its torch of humanism to everyone. It brings forth

---

[21] Roland Barthes, *Œuvres complètes de Roland Barthes,* Tome 1 (Paris: Seuil, 1993), p 147.

the humanity from those to whom all humanity is denied. Against the superficial silences and attentiveness that are always wrapped in boundless ignorance, West draws our attention to "these voices," not just to capture the power and beauty of their styles, but to hear their cries for freedoms and their calls to love, which condition a possibility of living together.

> If the blues is the struggle against pain for transcendence, then, as Duke Ellington proclaimed 'jazz is freedom.' Like Emerson, these great blues and jazz musicians are eloquent connoisseurs of individuality in their improvisational arts and experimental lives. Unlike Emerson, they sit on the edge of America's abyss—in the invisible chocolate infernos of the American paradise. Like Melville, they engage in deep-sea diving beneath the apparent American sunshine. Unlike Melville, they emerge with a strong blood-soaked hope and seductive tear stained smile. (*Democracy Matters*, pp. 91–92)

Thus, the blues is an energy that allows all outcasts to keep hope alive and affirm their being and their existence. The critical energy of the blues allows us to unearth the truth of the beings, West affirms. In light of this quote, the questions we can ask ourselves are as follows: How can African American art, in its diversity, conveyed by distinct individuals and not always with the same motivations, help in the reshaping of a more harmonious social life? How can it help people to get out of the cycle of violence? Can the victims of gratuitous violence use this art to build and rebuild themselves in a hostile environment? How can it encourage people to reinvest in everyday life whose multiple dimensions are not limited to aesthetic considerations?

Capitalism produces and exacerbates inequality and creates injustices. African American art can capture political, social, and economic disjunctions; find ways to lift society out of the cycle of violence and racism; and strengthen democracy. In his eyes, the blues challenges the abusive power and blind greed of an economic system that has lost control *(Tragicomique Amérique,* p.228).

The Westian hypothesis of the blues as a means of resolving conflicts is based on metaphors and analogies, the base (schemas, dispositions, habitus) of African Americans' sustained and privileged experiences. It shows that African American music is an inexhaustible source for meeting the complex and composite challenges of living together.

In fact, for West, the lessons of the blues people ensue from the following question: "How does one remain open and ready for meaningful solidarity with the very people who hate you?" He replies,

> Frederick Douglass and Bessie Smith, Ida B Wells-Barnett and Duke Ellington, Sarah Vaughan, Malcolm X and Martin Luther King Jr., Ella Baker and Louis Armstrong all are wise voices in a deep democratic tradition on America that may provide some clue to these crucial questions in our time. They all knew that even if the tears of the world are a constant quantity and that the air is full of our cries, we can and should still embark on a democratic quest for wisdom, justice and freedom. (*Democracy Matters*, p. 217)

By putting blues and jazz musicians in line with religious ones, West shows that blues is the umbrella under which all African American music is sheltered. Blues contains jazz, funk, soul music, gospel, R&B, rap, and slam poetry. To read West, at a time when capitalism is spreading and wreaking havoc throughout the world, African American art forms, more specifically blues and jazz, can serve as antidotes to the pathologies produced by this system.[22]

Certainly, West does not conceptualize the blues as a kind of power over all other music, but he shows that it is the locus of other musical languages that belong to the same ensemble. For example, when we have the blues, we can also sing jazz, soul, or rap. The blues is therefore the place where all other forms of African

---

[22] Cornel West, *Out There: Marginalization and Contemporary Cultures*, eds. Russell Ferguson, Martha Gever, and Trinh T. Minh-ha (Boston: MIT Press, 1990).

American music communicate; it is the music in which one can access the knowledge and the truth of all of America's Black people.

Blues is symbol, imaginary, and reality of all African Americans. But no matter how it is used, it takes us from a psychological state to reflection; that is, it moves from a logic of essence to a logic of meaning. The blues is a reference system that cannot be grasped if we do not have recourse to the nuances in this music's systems of symbolic meanings. Thus, in the Westian proposition "I have the blues, I sing the blues," I go from a passive situation to an active situation. The transition from humorous blues to lamentable blues is therefore a supposition that makes sense. We see that the blues has symbolic and real significance.

The transition from blues feeling to blues song is a moment when I give meaning to what's happening to me. "Having the blues" means recognizing one's state of health, depression, and therefore the realization of a lived reality, and "singing the blues" is trying to overcome this present situation by recalling the past, or even imagining the future. The blues is therefore both the African American's symptoms and cure. Given that America is the country where the outcast and "blues people" live, we will say that America is the nation of blues in every sense of the word, for it is simultaneously the dwelling of the outcasts and the creators: blues musicians. But can this country that is home of the blues hear the blues' call for understanding and rejection of hatred?

This is the fundamental question West asks. He thinks rightly or wrongly that the economic and political system cannot answer this call, for the logic of American capitalism is, he says, one of exclusion and nihilism. Blues invites you to meditate on yourself and on your relationships with others. Certainly, the musicians who perform solos express a need, a desire, a wish for acknowledgement, but they also acknowledge the presence of others.

It is the deep expression of humanistic values; a jazz or blues band is a place where we can perform a singular form of expression (the solo) in a moment of collective expression when all musicians must not only express what they feel but also express themselves in harmony with other musicians. So, when Marvin Gaye wonders "What's going on?" he is addressing the uncertainty and fear of police brutality, ghettos ravaged by drugs, the Vietnam War during which young people died, and he is inviting the love and tolerance of other.

Cornel West writes,

> In his song "What's Going On, Marvin Gaye invites peoples, black and white, yellow and brown—through these years of uncertainty and fear, to celebrate the ideological/theological feast of funk. This song is a protest against this planet ravaged by greed and waste. A political landscape of hopelessness. Yet hope come. Hope emerges from his gut-bucket black Christian faith. LIKE Marvin's ethereal suite of songs, that love does not deny calamity or scandal. It sees injustice, just as Jesus saw injustice, as a worldly reality to be transcended through a funky faith. Marvin calls this faith the "Wholly Holy." It is nothing more or less than the love ethos, the love that lasts forever, the love that leads us from darkness to light. (*Brother West: Living and Loving out Loud*, p. 76).

Blues is the breath of the African American people. With a sort of magical power, the blues musician binds the present to the absent, individual bodies to social bodies. Through the stories, legends, and realities they sing, African American musicians render visible the invisible. This is the case of James Brown's "I'm Black and I'm Proud" that all the invisible "Blacks" reclaim in their hearts.

Of this blues and jazz tradition that is R&B and funk, West will say that, like John Coltrane and John Keats, James Brown and Marvin Gaye understood the tragicomic condition of human existence. The dance moves and voices of Brown and Gaye express a call to listen to and acknowledge the Black experience in America; they are voices that express their humanism. Such is the spirit of funk (the fusion of rhythm and blues and jazz) according to West. Like laughter, dance and music are basic forms of freedom that no elite force has the power to eliminate. It is a language of conviction through which we tell the story of a people and of values.

Always recalling the matter of faith in African Americans' history, West shows that in his music, the bluesman expresses filiation, a relationship to the symbolic chain of social debt: debt to ancestors, community, and present and future generations; conversely, by showing that love of the other is fundamental, these African American artists make blues a constituent link of human relationships. This music, which defines the relationship to the elders, to oneself, to others, to circumstances, is therefore a relationship to the symbolic chain's whole. In other words, the blues shows that life is a system of generalized debt: Everyone is indebted to the community.

To better understand the meaning of the blues in relation to the debt issue, we must pay special attention to the former's rituals. The moment of musical expression is a moment of communion when each participant plays the role of actor and spectator. This interactive rite helps to neutralize differences and creates unity among participants.

During the show, the whole group is in fusion; it is a fraternity between the participants. More generally, what is revealed through the American blues experience are the stakes of all social life: the freedom and the means necessary to overcome daily misfortunes. Thus, having the myths and especially the rites that are at the heart of African Americans' practices and exchanges as favorite themes, the bluesman perpetuates the tradition. The blues "forge a mature hope that fortifies us on the slippery tightrope of Socratic questioning and prophetic witness in imperial America" (*Democracy Matters*, p. 216).

West adds,

> As infectious and embracing as the blues, we should never forget that the blues was born out of the crucible of slavery and its vicious legacy, that it expresses the determination of a people to assert their human value. The blues professes to the deep psychic and material pains inflicted on black people within the sphere of a mythological American land of opportunity. The central role of the human voice in this heritage reflects the commitment to the value of the individual and a speaking up about ugly truths. (*Democracy Matters*, p. 92)

Like Amiri Baraka, also known as LeRoi Jones, who shows how the bluesman expresses painful experiences through his playing, West shows how the "blues people" have transformed tragedy into hope; they did not get rooted in violence—hence the Westian concept of tragicomic. In other words, not to be rooted in a cycle of violent revenge, people make light of their tragic situation. West invites the American nation to use the experiences of African Americans, "the blues people." According to him, by reiterating the blues' chorus, America will recover from its illness and escape the cycle of violence and revenge. He writes,

> The blues, this black American interpretation of tragicomic hope, is rooted in a love of freedom. It proceeds from a free inquisitive spirit that highlights imperial America's weak will to racial justice. It is a sad yet sweet indictment of abusive power and blind greed run amok It yields a courage to hope for betterment against the odds without a sense of revenge or resentment. It revels in a dark joy of freely thinking, acting, and loving under severe constrains of *unfreedom*. (*Democracy Matters*, p. 216)

African American music is not just about entertainment; it makes use of entertainment. Blues and jazz in particular, which can be heard and played in the most remote corners of the globe, are ways for all the wretched of the earth to express their anger and their humanity, to resist the systems of domination and surpass them.

Faced with the unnamable, the unutterable (slavery, racial segregation, and injustice), Black Americans have always bounced back by transforming their pain, their anger, their tears and their shouts into love through the blues. In the same way, the blues makes it possible to slip from an individual experience to a collective one, and vice versa. It also makes it possible to pass from the status of receiver to one of emitter: internalization-externalization, such is the rhythmic tension in which the blues puts us.

The Rhythm of the Blues: The Contretemps

The rhythms of jazz and blues are rhythms of interdependence because the audience appropriates the rhythm propelled by the musicians, and vice versa. These rhythms transform the audience into actors. The musicians addressing their audience invite them to produce joy together for a moment. The musician establishes symbolic control of time that heals the uncertain and the unpredictable and allows one to rise above one's condition, be it poverty, wealth, race, or ethnicity.

And it is in accordance with the tensions that the rhythms' amplitude, directions, and speeds vary. If the jazzman often performs rhythmic "breaks" to influence the tensions, the bluesman chooses appropriate tones. The first offers *contretemps* to get us to listen to each other, and the second proposes tones for dialogue. We could say that blues and jazz provide methods for social compromise. Yet this search for compromise refuses any compromise of its principles, for the agreements through which the musicians express themselves must be contained in particular ranges. In the manner of jazz and the blues, the tones and rhythms of social exchanges must be free and in harmony. The tempo and tones that these musicians propose to their audience can be universalized.

Blues and jazz are American artistic and cultural experiences that can be extended to all the wretched of the earth. They open up toward the Other, so they are pathways to that which is universal. They are concepts that capture local and global experiences. Blues is a concept that transcends diversity on the one hand and provides methodologies (tone and rhythm) to strengthen democracy on the other hand. These musical forms invite the formation of groups without racial, ethnic, religious, or philosophical distinctions. The texts and sounds of the blues allow us to hear the sensibilities, words, and murmurs of all the world's marginalized populations. Though it is undeniable that blues musicians play for a particular audience, they let themselves be grasped and ask us to understand their performance in a kind of imaginative, dynamic, and interactive scheme.

America, country of the blues, must therefore take advantage of these musical forms that swing us in time and space and transport us to other cultures, to perform this exercise of otherness. But since the blues is also an expression of the lived experience, without surrendering its openness to the rest of the world, it first requires one to question one's own being: "Who am I?" From this interrogation, one is led to recognize the dignity of the other. All in all, the consequence of all Westian recourse to the blues is that if a human phenomenon is liable to multiple interpretations, it ultimately concerns all humanity. It is the meaning of this universal procedure of self-affirmation and acknowledgement of the other, this mode of appreciation of the social bond and revelation of truth, that we will also try to grasp in rap.

Rap, or the Youth's New Poetic Expression

The word "rap" refers to the acronym rhythm and poetry. Etymologically, the verb "to rap" means to strike a quick, sharp blow. It was used for the first time in the seventies by African American youth who lived in difficult conditions in the Bronx, a New York neighborhood. For these young people in these disadvantaged projects, rap is a form of musical expression that allows them to tell the story of their lives. As its name suggests, rap reminds the world of the "blows" that Black populations have suffered in history and that they continue to suffer today, particularly through the mass incarceration of Black youth.

Rap is the imprint of history, the derivative of Afro-American music, the warehouse of experiences. To produce their music, African American rappers use elements from multiple repertoires of other living or dead African American blues, jazz, funk, soul, R&B musicians, and "like every younger generation, our kids today see clearly the hypocrisies and mendacity of our society" (*Democracy Matters*, p. 177). The way in which youth express anger and disgust can sometimes change forms, but common denominators can be found.

Thus, rappers' words are produced from the sounds and melodies already created by other African American artists. It is as if they (the rappers) want to underline their cultural, social, and linguistic "kinship" or genealogy. Rappers perform a kind of recycling or recovery of other musical genres. But is this a form of recognition of the roles played by other musicians, or is it a commercial process, a strategy to enrich oneself? Why does this music interest the philosopher? For West, rappers are vanishing points, that is, points that evade the American academic and political structure.

Certainly, there are always remnants, elusive points, but one must first be aware of their existence and then have the will to grasp the maximum. Even if he does not say so explicitly, in trying to capture the vanishing points, West uses the deconstruction method provided by Derrida: "*le toucher*" (the touching).

Certainly, as Badiou says, "When you touch something or someone, you are that thing, but at the same time you are not," but this act creates at least proximity. Touch is the point of passage between the consciousness of being nonexistent and the existence of non-being.

This Westian approach resembles Paul Ricoeur's course of recognition; West believes that we must seek recognition, identification, and awareness of the existence of these excluded beings and offer them gratitude. Blues, jazz, and rap musicians are the ones who help him get closer:

> Like Emerson, these great blues and jazz musicians are eloquent connoisseurs of individuality in their improvisational arts and experimental lives. Unlike Emerson, they sit on the edge of America's abyss—in this invisible chocolate infernos of the American paradise.... Like Melville, they engage in deep-sea diving beneath the apparent American sunshine. Unlike Melville, they emerge with a strong blood-soaked hope and a seductive tear stained smile. They are the consummate American practitioners of the tragicomic. (*Democracy Matters*, pp. 91–92)

To better enter communion with this youth, West produces and interprets a rap record. By identifying himself at least for a moment as a member of their community, he happens, he says, to understand how this youth, an important fringe of the population, deconstructs the unthoughtful, the unthinkable in America.

According to West, to grasp this approach, ambitious deconstruction work is necessary. It is a question of first grasping the methods of deconstruction used by this youth themselves and then of deconstructing their "deconstruction." This requires that one bring the know-how of rappers and intellectuals face to face, and the best way to do that is to employ an interactive approach.

But the question one might ask oneself is whether, by overusing this interactive approach, the philosophy professor does not distance himself from the role expected of a researcher and a teacher? How can the production and musical interpretation of social facts in the company of musicians be used in academic research?

Cornel West writes,

> That such powerful poetry and insightful social critiques could be created by youths who have been flagrantly disregarded, demeaned, and demonized by the dominant market-driven culture-targeted as cannon folder by a racist criminal-justice system and a growing prison-industrial complex, in disgraceful schools and shattered families (including too many irresponsible, unemployed fathers) and violent environments—is a remarkable testament to the vital perspective and energy that can be injected into our democracy by the young, who have not made their compromises yet with the corrupted system. (*Democracy Matters*, p. 182)

Instead of rejecting rap, one must hear its critical examination of the political and social system and see how it can contribute to strengthening democracy and living together. In his eyes, young people who produce rap are very often rejected by the political class and intellectuals. However, it is not because they do not participate in political and intellectual activities that they are not total "beings." Not existing in a given universe does not mean to be naught, because naught corresponds to non-being, yet the nonexistent is. In other words, even if the rapper is nothing in the American academic or political world, they remain a being who exists in the artistic and cultural world.

The rapper produces knowledge and truths that inform society about the condition of beings. This production can enable leaders who are supposed to represent them to better design and apply policies regarding the youth. It is also an important source of knowledge for teachers and researchers.

But, he says, this is ignored by many political and academic leaders, including former Harvard University President Lawrence Summers, who accused him of interpreting and producing a rap record. He says that if the president of Harvard manifests such contempt for rap, it is because at the very least, he forgets that music is part of the "American dream," and that in the worst case, he ignores music's existential dimension. For West, rap allows for hearing the living presence of minorities' voices and drives inexistence into existence, nonbeing into being.

For the youth, rap represents that which is essential to recreate lost unity. It appeases social matters for the "nonexistent"; it is the place where young people freely express themselves in confidence and seek to bring their knowledge and know-how. They want adults to listen to them, to listen to their demands, and take into account their potentialities. It is the absence of this attention from adults that sometimes explains their behavior that some call deviant or even criminal. Admittedly, their postures, which could be perceived as excessive by an observer, are a way of filling a void, of attenuating a certain fear and anguish from an artistic point of view.

Cunning and subterfuge, sometimes on the verge of legality, constitute a way for these young artists to manage uncertainties and to make symbolic shifts in order to impose their existence. But what is the Westian interpretation of symbolic shifts?

To better explain this notion, let's take a detour to Josiane Boulad-Ayoub,[23] whose work invites a reflection on struggle and ideology (Agon and Symbolon). In fact, from a reflection on mimes

---

[23] Josiane Boulad-Ayoub, *Mimes et parades. L'activité symbolique dans la vie sociale* (Paris: l'Harmattan, 1995), 384.

and parades, that is, a culture's cultural forms and subjects, she proposes a general theory of symbolic activity, a particular theory of ideology, and a theoretical sketch of social structure.

She shows us that the symbolic configurations are organized, structured in economic, political, and cultural systems and sub-systems. According to their functions, these sub-systems are ordered to produce and organize social relations. Agonist activity, as an activity of struggle, allows one to see how individuals can be torn between their own convictions and the rules established by the group.

How does Boulad-Ayoub's analysis illuminate West's interpretations of African Americans' agonic and symbolic activities in general, and rappers in particular? How do these activities relate to the social structures and cultural productions of the concerned populations?

From West's point of view, artistic activities are both symbolic and agonic and serve as means of survival and meaning making. As we have seen, for him, the physical survival struggles of Blacks are carried out in a White supremacist ideological context. These ideologies unfold in all economic, political, and social fields. Thus, the agonic struggles are not dissociable from ideological struggles. Speech and the body complement and sometimes substitute each other in rap. Rappers' intellectual productions are inseparable from their physical practices.

Rappers always seek to make their prose aesthetic in order to be noticed. Very often, this approach is accompanied by a physical attitude. Through their verbal and physical performances that are related to social experiences, they show their language skills.

Like Chomsky,[24] let's say that, for West, there are two levels in the organization of rap language: the surface structure and the deep structure. The surface structure, which corresponds to performance, that is, to the phonological level (i.e., to the produced statement), determines the semantic interpretation, but it is the result of the

---

[24] Noam Chomsky, *Aspects of the Theory of Syntax* (Cambridge, MA: MIT Press, 1965).

deep structures' complex operations or transformations. Through their linguistic and corporal practices, rappers indicate their ability to reproduce and innovate.

In fact, whether it is in the ghettos or in less marginalized places, this youth shows through rap that they have practical control of the codes of the modernity to survive crises and even produce lucrative work. Through rap, they also demonstrate their mastery of derision techniques to deconstruct the discourse and structures that produced exclusions.

Rap or What Talking Means

The political, the social, a religious faith, a subjective thought, as well as the search for an aesthetic, a "beautiful ideal," are expressed in the rapper's lyrics. But this "beautiful" ideal is imagined in an "ideal" society, that is, a true society; in this sense, rap is an ethical code. It is true that when we listen to it, we do not just hear the lyrics; when we look at their music videos, we do not just see their gestures and their practices—we imagine the world to which they refer. Certainly, not everyone is referring to the same values, but everyone tries to express their convictions through orality.

According to Chomsky, language is governed by a large number of rules and principles that preside in particular over the order of words in sentences (syntax). Generative grammar, about which we are most often totally unconscious, is what he calls this set of rules that allows us to understand the sentences. Generative grammar has nothing to do with school grammar books, whose purpose is simply to explain what is grammatically correct or incorrect in a given language.

It must be recognized that in the Black American context, orality is a constitutive element of social existence. Mastering speech is essential to be considered a member of the group. With speech, Black populations show and use the resources of their lived experience and their imaginary to express, broadcast, channel, move, play, and refine through potentially infinite combinations, symbolic systems (sign systems, language, etc.) available to them. It is these same means that allow them to achieve through their art a kind of "totalization" of the economic, social, and cultural "fragmentation" they experience, on the one hand, and allow them to affirm their citizenship, on the other hand.

The meaning of practices, the dissemination of common knowledge, and the presence of ancestors are produced and conveyed through spoken language. Very naturally, therefore, rappers use language to construct their work and produce meaning. They do this by fashioning a style and implementing a discursive strategy. Rappers develop their poetry with syntax and semantics that are more or less their own but always inspired by the language of society's underworld. They extend the common language of the outcast by introducing meaning and thought.

Listening to the rapper, we can think of the statements of griots: "Since time immemorial . . . we are vessels of speech; we are repositories which harbor secrets many centuries old. The art of eloquence has no secrets for us . . . by the spoken word we bring to life the deeds and exploits of kings for younger generations" (Niane, *Soundjata ou l'épopée mandingue*, p.xx).

Depending on the speaker's charisma, speaking is either appreciated as an art, or it is not. The rapper who masters this art can take the listener toward all kinds of levels, scales, and different meanings of the world. The pathetic and/or poetic language of the rapper becomes a vital language for much of the youths who make it their own. For West, in general, rap is an imprint of the blues, itself the presence of gospel, the chant of slaves. Leaving one's mark on the melody of another, this is an "act of historical solidarity," as Barthes would say. But rap also allows us to understand how "invisible" people today try to confront the system that does not acknowledge them.

The Social and Political Significance of Rap

Through interactive experiences, rappers welcome the Other, musician or not, in their words and in their performances. For them, technological tools (the guitar, the computer, the microphone, or other instruments) can bring proximity to all beings, including the nonexistent. With their gestures and their postures, their words, their performance spaces, their roles in society, their representations, and their rituals, rappers show that the subject, even while caught in the grip of modernity and American capitalism, can hope for a better life.

In principle, rappers invite listening, compassion, and cordial understanding. They do it from a tone that expresses their feelings and offbeat rhythms. This rhythm imposes a cadence so that we hear the nuances of their voices and give the floor to others. With an extraordinary mastery of modernity's codes, these artists manage to slip into different modes of meetings, exchanges, associations, and confrontations with the system's proponents. Through their "scientific or technological" knowledge, these artists not only know how to control modernity, but also manage to control time and even impose their *contretemps*.

Through symbolism or semiotics, these artists reveal to us not only the truths that are intertwined in life and capitalist discourse, but also how, by using scraps, they divert and transform this system. The capitalist economic system crushes the "weakest," but by paying attention to artistic and symbolic productions, we can see how the "weakest" play and manipulate the system itself. The "prophetic" rappers manipulate the American system, inscribing their creations in the continuity of their culture. There is a kind of resistance to the onslaught of capitalism and a loyalty to their culture's sacred values.

Despite the American capitalist system's complexity and the multiplicity of artistic fields, rap is a musical form that applies to any action that can bring out the protest dimension. Rappers express their anger and their disappointments with virulent speech against the political and economic system that does not allow them to fully live out their citizenship. Certainly, "although hip hop culture has become tainted by the very excesses and amorality it was born in rage against, the best of rap music and hip-hop culture still expresses stronger and more clearly than any cultural expression in the past generation a profound indictment of the moral decadence of our dominant society" (*Democracy Matters*, p. 179). It is not simply through speech that these youths denounce the system's misdeeds; they also show it in their behaviors and bodily expressions.

The Place of the Body in Rap

The body is the place of symbolic struggles, the stake of which is the meaning to the world of the way one appropriates the world. By placing their bodies on stage, rappers also invite awareness of the outcasts' living conditions. Their physical posture and their speech are intended to generate reflection of outcasts' dehumanization. They seek to make forgotten beings visible.[25]

The way rap's musicians dress, including their way of wearing trousers and the absence of shoelaces, are all inspired by prison apparel. This style of clothing adopted by a good part of the youth today not only makes it possible to signify the prisoner's being, but also constitutes a means by which these young people maintain or even restore social bonds. The individual distinctive signs[26] are part of given social structures. In American society, where prisoners are generally considered nonexistent, by dressing like these prisoners, rappers show us that they are. Rappers remind us that the body is an experimental structure.

It is a storage place of *mobilizable* knowledge, "stock of knowledge at hand," as Schultz would say, to perform social practices. The rapper's body is not only a form that directs content (ideas), but it is, like a tattoo, a container in which we can give shape and color to ideas. The individual body is therefore a place of reception, *aestheticization*, and affirmation of existence.

For example, it is through their bodies that excluded populations that try to give themselves creative spaces and meaning to their lives. Indeed, during slavery, the only property America's African populations owned were their bodies. Today, the body is also one of the few places where the poor or prisoners can exercise their freedom. For some, their bodies are useless since they think they do not benefit from any consideration; for others it is the place of all possibilities: speaking, singing, eating, painting and dancing well.

---

[25] Cf. Cornel West, *Hope on a Tightrope: Words and Wisdom*.
[26] Cours Pratiques Culturelles des Africains Américains, Princeton University, 2010.

Thus, from the presumption that the body is useless, it ends up becoming everything. The body becomes the site of art. By emphasizing the centrality of the body in African American art, West invites us to revisit the history of this population and the social and economic reality they are currently experiencing. The centrality of the body also shows that the link to others traverses the link to oneself, because the other traverses oneself.

The use of the body is part of the quest for recognition. Those for whom the recognition of individuality is fundamental will go so far as to give their own bodies as a means to gain acknowledgement (*Hope on a Tightrope: Words and Wisdom*, 2011). This centrality of the bodies for the poor has not only the role of allowing creation, it is also a place of destruction and psychic violence (drug and alcohol use).

The Choice: Two Possible Routes

The rapper's posture on the public stage is ambiguous and even paradoxical. If some use their words and their bodies to assert their identities, others use them only to enrich themselves economically. The latter focus all their words on their bodies or those of women; others deal with the fragmentation, the rupturing of their community.

The former proclaims the dehumanization of beings loud and clear. They denounce the way in which America identifies, differentiates, and classifies itself, and classifies, differentiates, and degrades beings in accordance with the times. In any case, whatever their philosophy, when rappers speak, dance, play, or conspicuously spend their money, they settle their accounts with American society. In other words, West's analysis of the rapper's posture allows us to understand how the body that underlies both natural and symbolic activities is in fact a passive and active site of synthesis: a place of violence and oeuvres (music, dance, etc.).

Starting from these contradictions in rap, West updates the Duboisian notion of double consciousness. He extends it to all youths, even if, for him, it is especially those of the "chocolate cities," which must face the nihilism of some leaders. Indeed, in the "chocolate cities" where many systems of social integration are broken down, young people can only forge a promising future by using the little that the rest of society concedes to them.

When some turn to religion and spiritualism, others sink into materialistic logic; when part of this youth uses their individual body as a place of artistic expression, another party makes it a commercial object. Thus, the body and art become sites of unreasonable passions, materialism, and liberal economic thought. At the heart of the hip hop movement is a critique of the dogma of market fundamentalism and inequalities.

West wonders how this movement founded by young Blacks from the empire's chocolate cities first performed "ironically, their artistic honesty revealed subversive energy and street prowess in their work and life. As the entertainment industry began to mainstream their music, that street prowess became dominant—with the racist stereotypes of black men as hyper criminal and hypersexual and black women as willing objects of their conquests" (*Democracy Matters*, p. 181). But, fortunately, he notes, alongside a "wheeler-dealer," "market-oriented" hip hop, there is a generous, "progressive" hip hop that fights against injustice. As with Christianity, there are two streams in the hip hop cultural movement according to West: the ethical prophetic hip hop and the immoral Constantinian hip hop.

Constantinian Hip Hop

West says that Constantinian hip hop "revels in the fetishism of commodities, celebrates the materialism, hedonism, and narcissism of the culture (the bling! bling!) and promotes a degrading of women, gays, lesbians, and gangster enemies. In short, hip-hop is a full-scale mirror of the best and worst, the virtuous and vicious, aspects of our society and world" (*Democracy Matters*, p. 184).

> What a horrible irony it is that this poetry and critique could become co-opted by the consumer preferences of suburban white youths who long for rebellious energy and exotic amusement in their own hollow bourgeois world. But the black voices from the hood were the most genuine,

authentic voices from outside the flaccid mainstream market culture that they could find. So, the recording and fashion industries seized on this market opportunity. (*Democracy Matters*, p. 183)

By focusing all their marketing strategies on the violent and misogynistic aspects, the record industry has perverted hip hop.

According to him, it is the entertainment industry, especially the record majors who channeled this original energy to the market. "The companies perceived that white kids—72 % of those who buy hip hop CDs and even more who illegally download them—were much more interested in the more violence-ridden, misogynist mode than in the critical prophetic mode" (*Democracy Matters*, p. 181).

By making insult a means of identification, these Constantinian rappers feed on the difficulty of their community. They have no ideal or vision and do not respect the spirit of rap. This music, which is originally the expression of a furious disgust for the hypocrisy of xenophobic and racist adult culture, a disgust for egoism and capitalist inhumanity, has come to be perceived as macho, violent and commercial music. The "neo-soul movement' Jill Scott, The Roots, Kindred, Anthony Hamilton, Ruff Endz, Dru Hill, Donnie, India Arie, Alicia Keys—is a mellowing out of the roughness and toughness. Just as Gerald Levert, Aretha Franklin, Teddy Pendergrass, Stevie Wonder, Luther Vandross, Ronald Isley and R Kelly" (*Democracy Matters*, p. 183).

Prophetic Hip Hop

Prophetic hip hop is faithful to the ideals of justice. Embodied in the lyrics and rhythms of the first generation by Grandmaster Flash and the Furious Five, Kool Herc, Rakim, Paris, Poor Righteous Teachers, Afrika Bambaataa and especially KRS ONE, Chuck D's group, Public Enemy, and Outkast,

> it unleashed incredible democratic energies. Their truth telling about black suffering and resistance in America was powerful. The political giants of hip-hop all expressed and

continue to express their underground outlook of Outkast, righteous indignation at the dogmas and nihilism of imperial America. (*Democracy Matters*, p. 180)

As this Black music hailed from "'chocolate cities' with the giants of the next phase—Tupac Shakur, Ice-T, Ice Cube, Biggie Small et Snoop Dogg—linguistic genius and gangster sentiments began to be intertwined" (*Democracy Matters*, p. 181). This originally subversive music coming from the streets extended into vanilla (white) neighborhoods and around the world. But this expansion, which took place in a corporate logic, diminished the fervor of precursors. So while prophetic hip hop proclaims painful truths about their struggles and how their souls are wounded by rising unemployment and the explosion of drug markets, Constantinian hip hop promotes violence and sexism (*Tragicomique Amérique*, p. 197).

For him, like blues and jazz, prophetic hip hop allows for the inclusion of music in academic research because it is an undertaking that provides information on the cycles of happiness and misery that American youth experience. Prophetic hip hop draws attention to the presence of the Other, even if that Other is apparently absent, and asks us to have compassion for the weakest among us. It casts situations and characters that do not exist in the mainstream's field of vision.

Prophetic hip hop's position to inscribe the inexistent, to get closer to the marginalized, the "voiceless," the low income, the outcast, means that it does not sometimes have the commercial success it deserves. The music industry is doing everything to smother it and prefers to stage those who belong to the Constantinian stream of hip hop. Often without morality, Constantinian hip hop artists utter nothing but insults. The body, a woman's body, is only an object to be "bought."

LESSONS FROM AFRICAN AMERICAN ART

In a way, by making African American art a recourse against the American system's violence, West reconnects with Harlem Renaissance artists who radically opposed the capitalist and racist order. Let us remember the poetry of Langston Hughes or the novels of Claude McKay who, together with other intellectuals, sought to make the humanity of Black folk visible through art.

Through an in-depth analysis of the thoughts and works of Harlem Renaissance intellectuals and artists, West reflects critically on the art and political struggles of African American artists. He shows that these artists and intellectuals knew how to courageously deconstruct the discourse and images of guilt that the White supremacists sought to plaster onto the Black population in order to exculpate racist crimes and the transatlantic slave trade.

As such, he invites a more attentive reading of the Harlem Renaissance intellectuals' and artists' texts to sing the souls of these forgotten beings in unison. He refreshes their struggle to stand out to the outcast and invites all his fellow Americans to inscribe their actions in a future free of all barbarism (*Brother West: Living and Loving Out Loud*, 2009).

However, unlike the Harlem Renaissance intellectuals, he does not express his opposition to American politics with the poetry of innocence, but like them he uses his sufficiently powerful voice to pulverize the language of racists.

In fact, by placing himself in the continuity of the Harlem Renaissance, West uses the ambivalence of art, drama and laughter, and chiaroscuro, to hand political leaders' ambiguity back to them, and at the same time give hope to the hopeless. Art allows symbolic shifts between hopelessness and hope. His intellectual exploitation allows West to study society's immanent discourse. The blues, jazz, or rap expresses social, ethical, and cultural logic in specific ways.

All of these forms of music base their practices in all areas upon the substances that their world provides them. All these musical forms are ways of being, behaving, and defining oneself in society. They are not only means to reconcile beings, but also means to reconcile aesthetic and ethical categories and values. This double dimension, present in blues, rap, and jazz, represents a mode of appropriating and affirming the truth. And this can only be done with an offbeat rhythm.

According to West, the offbeat rhythm not only allows the rapper to highlight a symbolic control of the beat—since the offbeat itself may mean going against the normal beat—but it also allows him to show the reversibility of modernity's symbols. The offbeat rhythm allows those in the margins of industrial and capitalist American rationality to explore, from spatial-temporal elements, the means to escape. In other words, thanks to the offbeat, the "invisible" come, using the weapons of rationality to make their way to freedom, day by day. The offbeat allows the human being who is turning in a kind of circular vacuum to have points of reference to escape turbulence zones. It is through artistic productions that these populations express their blues, that is, their living conditions and their truths. They not only express their personal blues, but also listen to those of others.

This openness to others is, according to West, an invitation to reflect on the future of the individual and the collective from historical experiences. Bluesmen and jazzmen are the bulwarks who, with love and passion, help us discover and recover vital knowledge and wise ideas that lead to intellectual clarity and moral development (*Tragicomique Amérique*, p. 188).

By recounting the stories of the bluesmen who knew how to photograph American society in specific moments, and to highlight innovative solutions to crisis management, he shows how Afro-American music is a place of democratic expression, since in turns, everyone can express themselves and raise their voices (improvise) in harmony. Individual and collective salvation is found in jazz and blues. Society must soak up the blues and be inhabited by jazz. As these musical forms can never be destroyed, society can seek inspiration from them to strengthen democratic life. They also offer hope to the outcast.

Like the blues, African American music provides tragicomic hope but remains dangerous and potentially subversive. "Like laughter, dance, and music, it is a form of elemental freedom that cannot be eliminated or snuffed out by any elite power. Instead, it is inexorably resilient and inescapably seductive-even contagious" (*Democracy Matters*, p. 217).

The bluesman's and blueswoman's prophetic and artistic undertakings not only permit the recognition of all beings, but also constitute democratic sources. Thus, if America humbly uses the humanistic approach of bluesmen/women and prophetic religious figures, this could serve to consolidate international law and multilateral institutions, provided that this re-composition of a democratic America is made in a self-critical fashion. According to West, employing Socratic questioning on America is not sullying America, but rather recognizing the often-denied values of his people's historical struggles. The goal of Socratic questioning is democratic paideia (education)—the development of active and informed citizenship to preserve and deepen the democratic experience (*Brother West: Living and Loving Out Loud*, p. 202).

West writes,

> the Socratic love of wisdom holds not only that the unexamined life is not worth living but also that to be human and a democratic citizen requires that one musters the courage to think critically for oneself. This love of wisdom is a perennial pursuit into the dark corners of one's own soul, the night alleys of one's society, and the back roads of the world in order to grasp the deep truths about one's soul, society, and world. This pursuit shatters one's petty idols, false illusions, and seductive fetishes; it undermines blind conformity, glib complacency, and prophetic cowardice. Socratic questioning yields intellectual integrity, philosophic humility, and personal sincerity—all essential elements of our democratic armor for the fight against corrupt elite power. (*Democracy Matters*, p. 208)

West defines himself as a bluesman saturated with jazz. By defining his style from the world of blues and jazz, he seeks to combine his vision and ethics with an aesthetic. He invites us to understand from the inside how the African American population carries a burden, confronts mountains, tries to overcome visible and invisible walls, and seeks to show the presence of their ancestors. He says to be an Afro-American ... is to be in the situation, intolerably exaggerated, of all those who have ever found themselves part of a civilization which they could in no wise honorably defend—which they were compelled, indeed, endlessly no attack and condemn—and who yet spoke out of the most passionate love, hoping to make the kingdom new, to make it honorable and worthy of life. (*Brother West: Living and Loving out Loud*, p. 209)

African American art is a rebellious form of thinking that passionately calls out a civilization that continues to attack human dignity. But this posture hides another one: loving thy neighbor.

6

PROPHECY AND PHILOSOPHY

Whether it is his poetics or his writing techniques, West's style is recognizable by the double influence of religious prophecy and philosophy. His writing is an "archi-texture," that is, an intertwining of the fibers of American culture and the constituent elements of "world thinking's" organic tissue. His philosophical questions on the dialectic between the particular and the general, the local and the global, the collective and the individual, the multiple and the universal, lead him to take an interest in the religious and artistic fields.

He proposes a pragmatic approach that consists of identifying the implications and causes of the social facts in order to elaborate a thought. For him, it is about starting from religious beliefs and artistic productions to seek to reveal the truths that are sometimes hidden in social experiences. With West, art and religion are privileged realms in which one can find hints of truth and access the deep forces within oneself and other beings.

In other words, religion and art are privileged places to grasp the tension between immanence and transcendence on the one hand, and on the other hand, they allow seeing what individuals want to mean to the world and how their creations and creativity go beyond their personal experiences. They are places where the feelings of various populations unfold, areas where contradictions, conflicts, and modes of conflict resolution manifest themselves. From this point of view, they are not only means of effusion, they are also means of detection, of revelation of the truths buried in the individual and collective unconscious.

But the questions we might ask ourselves are these: How can opinions and religious beliefs be expressed through art? How can art, which is the place of expression of individual liberties, also be that of religion? How does one philosophize when one embraces a religious dogma and accepts that this dogma is the place of divine revelations?

For West, one does not exclude the other; one can be a philosopher and a believer, an artist and a prophet. The religious realm and the artist can express both their own and others' truths.

As for philosophers, they must not seek to produce truths, but must be content to seize them where they are. Certainly, to grasp these truths, West studies the American system, especially the place citizens explain their daily lives, but he deepens the study to go further and develop his vision of the Being. To do so, he finds support and frameworks from literature and anthropological historical, philosophical, economic, and sociological thoughts.

The questions that interest him are the following: How can one access the Being's truth when capitalism introduces questions, within the very collective and within the social, cultural, and ecological environment, that leave out the field of the Being's dignity? What methodology should one adopt when confronted with the enigma of becoming human?

In his eyes, if art and religion alone cannot gather the fragments of a quartered, ragged world, they do, however, indicate the modes of conflict resolution. That said, like the contradictions in the political system, there are issues of power. The disorientations deliberately traced by the political powers in America are those that he observes in the religious and artistic fields.

The misdeeds of capitalism's excesses in America are visible in all fields. But unlike the political and economic system that carries within it the residue of its slavery past and can only be destructive to humanity, some areas of art and religion can contribute toward a more harmonious social life. Art and prophetic religion have relegated the economic dimensions of trade to the background; they emphasize human values. Yet what escapes capitalism's logic is the human value of Beings, even if they are marginal.

Therefore, the vanishing point, the point that escapes capitalism's discursive imposition in America, is that of the humanity of beings, particularly the acknowledgement of the outcast's "Being." Philosophy as it is conceived, practiced, and taught in America, cannot capture these vanishing points, so West turns to continental philosophy and uses his cultural community's resources to philosophize. Faced with a number of questions, he turns to the thought productions of African Americans. Thus, his works appear offbeat. But let us remember he turns the offbeat rhythms of Afro-American music, including blues and jazz, into a rhythm of work.

AGAINST THE CURRENT OF ANALYTIC PHILOSOPHY

West feeds his thinking with substances of economic, political, and cultural life. It is in the cultural depths that he looks for the resources to express his thinking. For him, it is about seizing the truth from a dialectical approach, addressing it synthetically and making it intelligible. As such, he stands out from American analytic philosophy, which is essentially concerned only with logic and a priori forms of understanding.

In his book *Post Analytic Philosophy*, West questions the dominant analytic philosophy in the United States. In *The American Evasion of Philosophy: A Genealogy of Pragmatism*,[27] he issues a harsh and uncompromising critique of the teaching of philosophy in America in the face of what he calls logical positivism. While being part of American pragmatism, he distinguished himself from it by integrating the ideas of non-pragmatist thinkers like Blaise Pascal, Soren Aabye Kierkegaard, and the writer Anton Chekhov. In the same way, he enriches his approach by pushing religious and atheist thinkers to converse about philosophical foundations.

---

[27] Cornel West, *The American Evasion of Philosophy. A Genealogy of Pragmatism* (Madison: University of Wisconsin Press, 1989).

But it is in *Post-Analytic Philosophy*, prefaced by Lyotard, that Cornel West and Rajchman stand out most in analytic philosophy. Drawing on Richard Rorty, Donald Davidson, Hillary Putnam, and WV Quine, West and Rajchman show that it is imperative to detach from the dominant analytic philosophical movement in Anglo-Saxon countries to propose an approach that integrates European continental philosophy.

Jean-François Lyotard writes about this book:

> The essays that this book brings together bear witness to the vitality of American thought; not simply in the renewal of its links with its own singular tradition (which we could call "liberal," even if this word liberal would require a more precise theoretical elaboration), but also, on the basis of this singularity, its meeting with the traditions especially in Europe, I see in this book a number of signs of a reopening of the borders that Western intelligentsia has divided for two centuries. This book also announces the stakes of the issue of postmodernity.[28]

And Jacques Derrida adds,

> Through the internal differences and divisions of the collected essays, which also constitute (its) richness, I am convinced that something essential is fully revealed in this collection of articles; which, in fact, is new to thought in North America today. This event is important in itself in the United States, but I think it is also adapted to transform the space of philosophical exchange with continental Europe, especially, with French thought. Indeed, I believe this book, with rigor and lucidity, contributes to a transformation that has already begun.[29]

In the book, West argues for a critical and uncompromising interpretation of academism, politics, and culture. He also wants

---

[28] West, Cornel, and John Rajchman. *Post-Analytic Philosophy*, p. 14 (New York: Columbia University Press, 1985).

[29] Cornel West, et John Rachjman, *La pensée américaine contemporaine* (Presses universitaires de France, 1991). Commentaire de Jacques Derrida.

the philosophical dialogue to be inclusive, to agree to converse with those at the margins of society. In his text on the politics of American neo-pragmatism, West considers that it is from the ruins created by American capitalism that the philosopher must develop their thought. He blames modern America for the disappearance of true social bonds. He also blames it for the dehumanization of its people, especially through ultraliberal policies.

However, he does not limit himself to criticism of public policies; he also reviews the social relations in his community as well as interracial and intercultural relations. He publishes *Race Matters* in 1993 (a bestseller with more than four hundred thousand copies sold), which propels him to the forefront of the American media and intellectual scene. *Newsweek* salutes the author's elegant prophetic prose. The *New York Times* says this book is fierce and a rigorous moral critique.

It must be said that in *Race Matters*, West shows how the question of African Americans matters in the way the entire United States thinks and acts in the world. He invites intellectuals to consider, inter alia, the contribution of religious prophecy in strengthening democracy. He defends the access of the poor and the excluded to public services so that they regain their dignity and their civism. He also invites intellectuals to reassess the contribution of art to the self-determination of African American populations. But he does not stop there. He criticizes not only religious fundamentalism that leads to nihilism, but also racism, including the pernicious role that White supremacy has played in thwarting democracy's development in America. For him, because of the physical and psychological violence suffered, the lives of Black people in the United States are different from those of all the peoples of the world. No other Black people have endured so much after slavery, the terror of Jim Crow. To control and exploit Blacks in the United States, White supremacists infused Blacks with corrosive and insidious forms of self-destruction.

Whether they are "liberal structuralists" or "conservative behavioralists," they all ignore the nihilistic threat to Blacks in America, he says: "The liberal doesn't want to talk about culture because it takes attention away from government programs. The conservative focuses on values, ignores political-economic realities, and denies victimization" (*Democracy Matters*, p. 171).

The questions these politicians should ask themselves are these: How do these populations cope with social despair? Why does part of this group have low self-esteem? How do they not stay depressed or in depression?

For West, capitalism that values materialism leads to hyper-materialistic consumer madness in the American populace. The materialism that nurtures and defines American culture weakens all the collective defense mechanisms of populations, especially African American ones. And on the individual level, the materialism that leads the weakest to the loss of all hope, confidence, and psychic and spiritual health also leads to self-destruction. Thus, he says, the suicide rate is steadily rising among Blacks in America. In short, unregulated capitalism is literally killing the bodies, minds, and souls of Black people.

In the past, he recalls, African American populations have been able to create cultural buffers such as churches that have valued service and solidarity within African American communities: Each person looks out for the other and takes care of the group. While some of these structures continue to fulfill these missions, many have been misled by unscrupulous leaders. He repeats everywhere in the media that these dishonest African American elites are a danger to their community and to the American nation.

In *Race Matters*, he denounced the lies and the dangerousness of these Black elites. With respect to the Clarence Thomas case,[30] he says that by refusing to tell the truth, many Black leaders fell into the "pitfalls of racial rationalities." Faced with the accusation of sexual harassment against this judge, many Black leaders tried to close ranks in the name of so-called total solidarity. According to West, no Black leader was willing to say in public that this candidate

---

[30] Clarence Thomas, named by George H.W. Bush as a candidate for the Supreme Court of the United States, was charged with sexual harassment by a woman named Anita Hill.

for the Supreme Court was not qualified for the position. On the contrary, they all overwhelmed Anita Hill, who accused Thomas of having sexually harassed her, which leads people in a racist nation to believe that, with regard to communitarian issues, the African American world is ready to sacrifice, or even develop, a culture of absolute subordination of Black women.

Starting from this legal case, West proposes that America conduct a public debate on the question of gender and sexuality in American society. He says there is a need to publicly debate this issue, which is often discussed behind closed doors. According to him, one of the key questions regarding the problem of race is that of gender and sex, in particular of the "alleged" sexuality of Blacks.

In fact, this question refers to an analysis of the methods and strategy of domination still employed by nihilists. This is an essential question if we want to understand racism. The search for optimum methods to control individual and collective bodies has always preoccupied capitalists, particularly nihilists. For capitalists, the control of the body is necessary for their work of exploitation, and for the nihilists, the control of the body through sexuality can strengthen their power and methods of societal domination. Control of the individual body engages in control strategies of the social body. These strategies and mechanisms of enslavement are still relevant.

As can be seen, West feeds his analyses with materials provided by both his country and his community. As we have said, interracial and intercultural relations are a breeding ground from which he seeks to philosophize. For him, if Black America wants democracy to triumph, it must dare to criticize itself and not develop a complex. The lack of discernment, humility, and indignation of a large portion of Black leaders shows that the African American community is not homogeneous; it undergoes class and rank struggles. In fact, according to West, there are three types of Black leaders:

- Black leaders who deny racism or race, with remarkable political know-how; this type of leader proliferates.
- Black leaders who play on racial identification and are the brokers of White power.

- Black leaders who transcend racial issues. They are prophetic leaders with genuine vision and courage, such as Jesse Jackson in the 1988 election.

Depending on the category, we do or don't play with racial tensions. But to fight racism, we must fight against all forms of injustice. In this sense, even though affirmative action laws are insufficient, they are necessary in the struggles against injustice. However, in the face of poverty, social justice can only be achieved on the basis of voluntarist and just policies. This approach also implies understanding and empathy toward the low income.

Generally, for West, we must fight against all forms of injustice and recognize the humanity of all beings, including of those we do not see: the outcast. Especially since the political elites and the plutocrats marginalize these populations, the latter, despite all the forms of violence they undergo, manage to create spaces to give meaning to their life and re-create social bonds (*Race Matters*, 1993).

It is from these public spaces of tugging and productions of meaning that West brings pragmatism into play. He wonders how we can think about justice when we do not put all citizens on the same level of equality before the law. How can the left-behind get by if we simply limit ourselves to the prescriptions of principles without support?

Before answering these questions, let us say, with West, that citizenship has this peculiarity of not only placing itself in the perspective of subjects as mere consumers, but also of showing that they are Beings who have an identity to affirm.

Pragmatism

According to the Larousse dictionary, "pragma," from its Greek origin (*pragmatos*) means "fact," and pragmatism refers to an attitude of someone who adapts to situations. Pragmatic people are action oriented. As a philosophical doctrine, pragmatism consists of taking practical value as a criterion of truth. For example, in analytic philosophy, in which there is a great deal of interest in languages, pragmatism in linguistics consists of studying the relationship between language and its use by speakers in a communication situation. In other words, linguistic pragmatism studies presuppositions, innuendos, conventions of speech, and so forth.

Thus, in an America characterized[31] by racial questions with injustices of all kinds, philosophizing does not only seek to grasp truths in the cultural, artistic, and religious productions of populations, but also to provide exploratory and operational concepts to analyze the experiences. In doing so, West shows that the articulation modalities of religious, aesthetic, and political language must be done by taking into account the pragmatism developed by Charles Sanders Peirce, William James, John Dewey, Emerson, Richard Bernstein, Morton White, Richard Rorty, with contributions from Sidney Hook, W.E.B. Du Bois, and C. Wright Mills, in the hope of a more harmonious social life.

From the pragmatism of Charles Sanders Peirce,[32] he retains the mental experimentation method, a method that helps to form exploratory hypotheses whose verification can lead to their confirmation or denial. This method, which also serves as the theory of inquiry, provides conceptual clarity. He also retains from Charles Sanders Peirce's thinking the importance of beliefs, for they allow for the understanding of habits that lead to actions.

In this perspective, West salutes John Dewey's theoretical contribution in the democratic debate, including his contribution to "social liberalism." Like Dewey, he believes that politics must participate in self-realization in democracy. Indeed, if democracy allows for conflict management, and if its purpose is ethics,[33] then the pragmatic approach confirms that ethics is the foundation of democracy, and it is a *sine qua non* of freedom.

---

[31] Cornel West, *The American Evasion of Philosophy* (Madison: University of Wisconsin Press, 1989).
[32] Joseph Brent, *Charles Sanders Peirce: A life*, 2nd edition (Indianapolis, Indiana University Press, 1998).
[33] Elizabeth Anderson, "Dewey's Moral Philosophy," *Stanford Encyclopedia of Philosophy* (2005).

As for the neo-pragmatism developed by Richard Rorty, West both agrees with but also somewhat distances himself from it. Like Rorty, he thinks that it is not because there are "epistemological confusions" in pragmatism that it must be rejected in bloc. For example, pragmatism's anti-essentialism makes it possible to demolish racial or even racist ideologies. West says that pragmatism allows people like him, coming from minority groups, to challenge hegemonic representations while suggesting ways to avoid confrontation. But he says he disagrees with Rorty's affirmation that all references to God must disappear from political life and only secular terms like *republic*, *democracy*, and so forth must be maintained. He also disagrees with John Rawls's belief that religious discourse is potentially dangerous.

Indeed, though Rorty and Rawls support the rights and freedoms, including religious ones, of all citizens, they both want the removal of religious discourse from the public sphere. For West, "the liberalism of influential philosopher John Rawls and the secularism of philosopher Richard Rorty—the major influences prevailing in our courts and law schools—are so fearful of Christian tainting that they call for only secular public discourse on democracy matters" (*Democracy Matters*, p. 160). This radical secularism that opposes all religious language in the public sphere is exclusive, yet democracy must be inclusive. Certainly, though religion can be a source of conflict, it can also contribute to a better social life.

In his view, the proposals of Rawls and Rorty are not without wisdom, but they deliberately ignore how certain religious beliefs can reinforce the respect of democratic norms. He wonders

> Should he—or we—remain silent about these convictions when we argue for our political views? Does personal integrity not require that we put our cards on the table when we argue for a freer and democratic America? In this way, Rawls's fear of religion—given its ugly past in dividing citizens—asks the impossible of us. Yet his concern is a crucial warning. (*Democracy Matters*, p. 160)

According to West, capitalism and democracy in America lead to a stalemate. By considering solely material bases, America ends up no longer seeing the Being in its entirety. In seeking to reconstruct in its entirety the Being that has been fragmented by capitalism, West turns to religious discourse, including prophetic Christianity.

He believes that in order to advance democracy and improve people's living conditions, we must take into account sensitivities, traditions, and practices, but also put in place a rational system. In this perspective, religion is not necessarily antinomy to democracy. It is only necessary to distinguish progressive branches from the reactionary ones.

To transform social structures in America through political action, it is necessary to connect the progressive branch, meaning the prophetic tradition of Christian thought, reason, and Marxist social criticism. This theoretical framework, which combines the American pragmatist philosophical tradition, Marxist criticism, and Black liberation theology, will make it possible to elaborate a rational and universal tool of emancipation that he calls prophetic pragmatism.

Very often in radical innocence, African Americans have known how to use religion to manage their uncertainties by smashing White supremacist attitudes and devices that have tried to constrain their humanity. They have used this religion to deconstruct and cripple the mechanisms of individual or collective physical, psychological, even religious oppression of these supremacists. West seeks to show how the process of American capitalism's theoretical and practical construction, inside and outside of America, is developed in Constantinian Christianity and not in prophetic Christianity.

Prophetic Christianity permits the deconstruction, the overflow, the expungement, and the clean-up of religion's pollution. This Westian position could be considered part of an ideological struggle. But how could he who intensely experiences the suffering and distress of his African ancestors transported as slaves to America bring out this unspeakable truth in his works? He even makes this truth one of the pillars of his philosophy to deal with the human condition. However, he does not limit himself to circumscribing the truth of his ancestors' suffering only in racist America; he extends it to all the different components of American society.

By using the tools of prophetic Christianity and philosophy to develop his thinking, West opens up a new area of research. Indeed, if in religious prophecy and pragmatism there is the presence of meaning, of thought, of the Being, then West opens up the possibility of developing common knowledge and scientific thought. For him, the pragmatism associated with the religious prophecy he calls "prophetic pragmatism" can only strengthen living together. But what does prophetic pragmatism consist of? Before taking an in-depth look at the meaning of prophetic pragmatism, we will outline the status, role, and place of prophecy in general for West.

Prophecy: Contributions and Limits

In the American context, where Christianity plays an important role in the lives of citizens, the aspiration to a democratic ideal is grounded in religious beliefs. From this point of view, prophetic Christianity can help to set the conditions for living together. West rereads the Bible to extract the possibilities of social harmony.

Biblical exegesis allows him to see how Black populations in America have been able, in different places and at different times, to resist and to reconstitute and affirm their being. He carefully examines how these populations were able to renew their identity struggles and think about themselves through their religious beliefs and practices. Far from being defeated by life's circumstances, Black people have found how to make their experienced cycles of happiness and distress clear and visible through religion. In *Democracy Matters*, West evokes the ravages of the Amerindian genocide; the crushing of workers' lives by the inhuman machinery of capitalist excesses; the massive oppression of women, homosexuals;

and the deeply undemocratic and dehumanizing hypocrisies of White supremacy.

In fact, one cannot understand the prism of the fight against racism in religious prophecy as it is conveyed by the Black Baptist Church in general, and by Martin Luther King Jr. in particular, unless confronted with African Americans' despondency:

> The especial aim of prophetic utterance is to shatter deliberate ignorance and willful blindness to the suffering of others, and to expose the clever forms of evasion and escape we devise in order to hide and conceal injustice. The prophetic goal is to stir up in us the courage to care and empower us to change our lives and our historical circumstances. (*Democracy Matters*, p. 115)

It is evident that prophetic Christianity not only raises hope, but also uses critical reason and courage to transform social relationships. Therefore, if Christians in America appropriate these values of prophetic Christianity and use critical reason, democracy can only be strengthened (*Tragicomique Amérique*, p. 34)

Since in the real world prophecy can have consequences in people's lives, the identification of its practical implications can help individuals to break free. Hence, instead of substituting prophecy for philosophy, and pragmatism for abstraction, West makes them complementary through an innovative approach. This allows him not only to provide tools to analyze and evaluate the American political and economic system, but also to propose ways out of discord.

Indeed, the prophetic word calls for understanding, dialogue, and transcendence. It is a pragmatic approach that allows individuals to listen to each other. It is more suited to symbiosis than to dichotomy. Prophetic African American Christians teach us the reality of America from the inside.

Moreover, religious prophecy makes it possible to inscribe alongside ontological freedom—that is, that of one's being itself—the social freedom relating to the relation to others. The values of prophetic Christendom are subversive: If everyone is created in God's image, a certain idea of egalitarianism can evolve. Consequently, updating the norms of religious prophecy can prevent the corruption of democracy and justice. The individual who has "sinned" is invited to undergo a psychic conversion. With respect to America's bloody history, psychic conversion consists, for example, of inviting the rulers to convert, to carry out their self-criticism, in the name of God and all his attributes. In a pragmatic way, we see how prophecy opens up paths to love, peace, and justice on the one hand, and on the other makes it possible to grasp the contradictions and differences between the running of institutions and people's real lives.

The philosophy that is concerned with pragmatism seeks to understand how ideals are action oriented and how they work and can function in social life. West defines this way of philosophizing as prophetic pragmatism: a method and way of thinking that allows us to see the real and practical consequences of prophecy in the world. He combines religious, particularly Baptist, prophecy and the Emersonian tradition of philosophical criticism and emancipatory action. Since emancipation first consists of intellectual emancipation, he invites his fellow citizens to reclaim the true values of religious prophecy, which contain critical reasoning, to evaluate their forms of communal and individual life. Such an approach, it must be admitted, is contrary to academic thought. By integrating the prophetic tradition of Christian thought, reason, Marxist social criticism, and Black liberation theology into his approach, West not only builds a theoretical framework that allows him to develop a concept—prophetic pragmatism—but also to convey certain prophecies in the field of philosophy.

For him, what is missing in American philosophy is attention to the essential dimension of religious prophecy. He thus seeks to inscribe prophecy in the field of philosophy and to relatereligious practice to artistic practice. He therefore seeks to bridge the gap between philosophy and theology, on the one hand, and, on the other, between orality (prophecy) and writing (philosophical texts). What is generally lacking in pragmatism is that it does not take into account the essential dimension of religious prophecy.

Certainly, religion as a system of beliefs and practices for groups of people contains enormous logical contradictions, but it is also the place where human beings try to find answers to their condition. Some even make it a way of life. Religion's prophetic dimension helps them turn experienced tragedy into hope. This is a prophecy steeped in blues, that is, tragicomedy.

A Prophecy Steeped in Tragicomedy

Tragicomedy is the ability to laugh at experienced tragedies in order to endure pain. Prophecy steeped in tragicomedy hears people's pains, dramas, tragedies, and sorrows. But how can one express people's truths using prophecy as a reference? Doesn't prophecy itself lead people to resignation? How do we consider freedom from the standpoint of prophetic pragmatism? How do we philosophize with prophecy?

For West, prophecy is not a substitute for philosophy; it is an object of philosophy. It concerns the realms of the world of ideas and the palpable world. As such, the philosopher can and must be interested not only in prophecy but also in pragmatism.

Blues-soaked prophecy does not simply express transcendent truth for West. It allows us to tell others' truths precisely because the blues implies listening to the other. Inspired by the blues, prophecy goes against the beat, sometimes even against the current of the "traditional" prophecy. But could it be otherwise, when one knows that prophecy is often at the service of liberation?

By inscribing prophecy in the tones and rhythms of blues and jazz, West provides a framework for theoretical analysis to concretely reflect on the social world. Moreover, by integrating the prophetic tradition into the bluesman's practice, he manages to show how the musician's approach engages in a spiritual or religious life. This approach is off the beaten track.

It is not a matter of using religion and art to get lost in an aestheticization or pathos of the human condition, but to use it to reflect upon freedom. Prophetic pragmatism allows him to not only question what society is about, but also question how society wants to be: free. Thus, the representations of blues and jazz groups are privileged places where all the feelings of the African American populace are expressed:

> The blues philosopher is the teller of the tales and the singer of the songs that keep alive the best of our historical legacies. Such inheritances sustain our courage to think critically about the past and act compassionately in the present and offer an alternative future. In this way, the bluesman descends from both the griot tradition and the prophetic tradition. *(Brother West: Living and Loving out Loud*, p. 180)

These musical forms express exceptional living conditions. They simultaneously keep us informed of African American institutions' stability and permit the expression of all novelties. They are therefore sites of truths, places where one can grasp the elements closest to Black people's lives.

In their concerts, bluesmen and jazzmen trigger a course of truths with their music. Their improvisations supplement the situation itself. As Badiou (1989) would say,

> This supplement is neither assignable nor representable by the resources of the situation (its structure, the established language which names its terms, etc.). The emotion of the music is so strong and contagious that something extra-musical is happening. The Blues is a singular naming of the lived experience and the putting into play of a signifier.[34]

If philosophy has the specific challenge of providing a unified conceptual space for event naming that serve as a starting point for

---

[34] Alain Badiou, *Manifeste pour la Philosophie* (Paris: Les Editions du Seuil, Collection l'Ordre Philosophique, 1989), 19.

truth procedures, then West is entitled to speak about the prophetic figures of the jazzman or bluesman, such as Louis Armstrong or John Coltrane.[35] About Coltrane, he writes,

> His vocabulary was different, but his sonic attitude—now joyful, now mournful, now playful, now serious—was similar. You can't listen to Trane and not feel the tragic dimension of the stories he tells. "Alabama", for instance, the composition he wrote to memorialize the four young precious black girls killed in the September 1963 bombing of the Sixteenth Street Baptist Church in Birmingham, ranks alongside the speeches of Martin Luther King Jr, whose poetic cadences had such a deep influence on this jazz musician. (*Brother West: Living and Loving out Loud*, p. 123)

He adds, "Like Shakespeare or Chekhov, Trane's work gave a narrative rhythm to our human tragicomic condition. Just as playwrights turned that condition into drama, he turned it into sound" (*Brother West: Living and Loving out Loud*, p. 123).

Jazz and blues reveal themselves as vehicles to express the human condition, which is why the philosopher can use them to think about truths. As Badiou might say, it is a conceptual site where generic procedures are reflected on. In other words, we find forms of prophetic expression in jazz, hence the Westian concept of prophetic blues or jazz.

MARTIN LUTHER KING OR PROPHECY IN MINOR KEY

From musical and religious expressions, West gives new meaning to the notion of prophecy. Martin Luther King Jr. embodies the prophecy, or the political thought, of an underlying minority, what the philosopher Stéphane Douailler calls prophecy in minor key.

---

[35] Musical compositions by John Coltrane, which commemorated the four Black girls killed in September of 1963 by a bomb placed in the Baptist church on Sixteenth Street in Birmingham.

In other words, as in jazz and blues, from a given structure, King offers a particular tone to express a people's feelings and lived experiences. He brings an essence to prophecy that is generally detached from people's lives. Dr. King lowers and raises to their heights the thoughts that echo the timbre of the people's voices.

Indeed, West thinks that Reverend King embodies the experiences of the African American conceptual and romantic figure. In other words, King is the emblematic figure of the Black struggle. His dedication to the Black cause explains why a large part of this community gave him their absolute trust. In all fields, the members of the Black community have appropriated the reverend's prophecies. Blues musicians see him as a blues-soaked prophet.

The prophet imbued with the blues' musical movement is interested in the blues, conditions, and truths of the Other. He resembles the bluesman soaked in prophetic values, who invokes love of one's neighbor, peace, democracy, justice, and the freedom of Beings. By juxtaposing the figure of the prophet to that of the bluesman or jazzman, West carries out original work on the dialectic of within and without, of the individual and the collective, of the specific and the general. Churches and music groups are places where the tension between one and many can be grasped; they also show us how to resolve conflicts. American democratic life needs the blues' rhythms and the rapper's social critique, all harmonized by King's vision.

The bluesman is a pacifist, the rapper is anti-establishment, and the prophet is a wise man; they are all "pragmatic rebels." Therefore, if we listen well to the truths they gather and restore, we can collectively sing a people's blues together and aspire to a better society. Let us remember that for West, singing the blues while having the blues is not celebrating the symptom of weakness, but rather a way to rebound. The blues, like King's prophecy, allows people to exist and to reach out to each other.

Thus, to prophesize in the tones of the blues and in the rhythms of jazz is to listen to others' blues, hear their truth and condition, and then comfort them. Likewise, playing music in the spirit of prophecy is inviting others to love. Prophecy and African American music are complementary. Both are forces of remembrance and hope. The artist is not devoid of vision and ideal, and the prophet is not a being who is detached from reality and hears only God. A prophet also hears others' truths.

For this reason, King is an example. West writes,

> The legacy of Martin Luther King Jr. is the culmination of not only the democratic tradition in the USA but also the humanist tradition of Socrates and Jesus—Athens and Jerusalem. Needless to say, King is a Christian bluesman of the highest order! Like him, I try to be a prisoner of hope, a fanatic of fairness, and an extremist of love. (*Brother West: Living and Loving out Loud*, p. 210)

This quote shows that even though King embodies Christianity, his thinking goes beyond this religion. He appears as a universal figure that other religions appropriate.

Indeed, King seizes the fragmentary and discontinuous truths that arise from events and relates them to other truths that come, according to him, from God. But this conception does not isolate him in bigotry or in an attitude of exclusion. There is a great spirit of tolerance within him. He thus appears as a secular figure. According to West, for King, it does not really matter whether these truths are material or spiritual, revealed or not, demonstrable or not; the essential thing is to show their production conditions and their coherence or their logic. Like bluesmen, King seizes singular truths to extend them to the whole world. King's thoughts, like those of the blues, are transcendent thoughts. They reveal truths that go beyond the group's experiences. They are also generic thoughts, since the individual performance of actors within the collective supposes a multiplicity of truths ad infinitum.

As with blues and jazz bands, in which every musician is given a moment to improvise, King expresses himself, improvises, and raises and makes his voice heard in the meetings. Musicians, like prophets, manifest their truth and their freedom, which is never achieved. Like the music scene, the Church is a jam session venue.

It is a space where not only do we improvise, but also one where we update lived experiences that transcend and cause other truths to flourish.

In the segregationist context in which individuals are separated and isolated, the prophetic call for a collective project constitutes a subversive act. Like the bluesman in front of his audience, blues-soaked prophecy invites the public to be active and not passive.

7
ACTIVISM AND THE POETICS OF COMMITMENT

For West, anyone who is in love with the spirit of freedom and justice cannot be indifferent to the social and economic situation of the people in the United States. In fact, according to him, many people are in poverty because of some influential members of the American elite. It is therefore important to change the system. To do this, we must engage in societal life. But though political commitment is a necessity, it is also important to reflect on the ways and means of a harmonious life. These terrains are a laboratory for analyzing social facts from a historical and social perspective.

It is less a question of reproducing what we see, what is shown to us, in writing, than seeking to push to the fore what is hidden and often escapes us. How do we establish and guarantee the durability of a democratic system when the dysfunctions of the collective management and administration systems do not meet the requirements of solidarity and of a harmonious life? How do we allow for the affirmation of each individual's identity without falling into a radical otherness? What will happen to future relations between these individuals in an ultra-modern world characterized by the exclusion of large segments of society? It is by answering these questions that West develops his poetics, his philosophy of engagement, and his activism.

According to West, emancipation can only be achieved by acknowledging the humanity of all Beings. Such acknowledgement implies that we encroach on the division of sensitive space and that we discuss the vision, understanding, and discourse with respect to common objects: public spaces and goods. In other words, we must seek to emancipate ourselves from the gaze of others and to leave the places to which we have been relegated. Like Jacques Rancière,[36] West thinks there is a distribution crisis of places and functions in the community. He is interested in the part of the "no-parts."

Indeed, the system of divisions that defines people's respective parts and places unjustly sets the common shares and the exclusive shares. However, a large number of citizens, especially precarious workers, do not have the time and tools to take advantage of the common space. These people cannot exercise their rights because most of them do not have access to the education system, and sometimes even well-educated people are discriminated against. The challenge of politics is the fight against unfair systems of division and distribution.

It is necessary that those who have the competence to understand these issues, especially intellectuals, get involved in social and political movements to help citizens left to the margins reclaim the common space. For this to occur, we must first look at the sources of discord.

According to West, it is the systemic implementation of forms of nihilism and physical, moral, and symbolic violence that destroys any possibility of living together. While the American populace has always been able to oppose the violence, these reactions have often not lived up to the democratic stakes. The question, therefore, is why have so much momentum and so many democratic currents been annihilated in the history of this great country? How do we anticipate the future of a nation when part of the population is used as "raw material"?

The strength of capitalism lies in its ability to accommodate insidious forms of domination and nihilism on the one hand and to conform to systems that do not call its dynamics into question on the other. However, the status quo's effects are negative with respect

---

[36] Jacques Rancière, *Le Spectateur Emancipé* (Paris : La Fabrique, 2010); *Aux bords du Politique* (Paris : Gallimard, 1998); *La mésentente* (Paris: Galilée, 1995).

to the social contract since the former does not allow for the substantive reforms necessary for democratic dynamism. And nihilism, whether produced by White supremacists or by minorities, locks the American people into negative identities that lead to racism. Moreover, the refusal of any adversarial debate and of any fight for justice and transparency allows nihilists to disguise the truth and satisfy their plans.

It is therefore crucial and urgent to fight these different forms of nihilism and their false justifications at the political, ethical, intellectual, and cognitive levels. West pays particular attention to the ideologies and religious beliefs that are at the core of the manipulation of the political system.

THE DECONSTRUCTION OF THE IDEOLOGIES AND MECHANISMS OF ALIENATION

For West, if the umbilical cord that connects politics to religion has officially been cut, there is a close link between these two domains. In fact, he shows that religion is present in politics, and politics is present in religion.

To get us to grasp the political stakes in religious practices, and vice versa, he raises the following questions: What, beyond economic logic, enables the efficiency of American capitalism? How do we study the symbolic domain of the American system's domination? How does American society portray itself?

We can only grasp this complex structuring of domination if we try to elucidate the myths that found these dogmas in American capitalism. To do this, West analyzes political, economic, and religious rites, because ritual is a myth in action he says. To understand what led to the establishment of the present order of things, he sifts through the dogmatic beliefs that America is God's chosen one. He shows that this vision of America, the foundation of its isolationism, is not new.

In other words, the politico-religious rites are dramaturgical remakes of founding events. West carries out a kind of archeology of capitalism in America by referring to the topography of current social and economic situations. While deciphering religious texts,[37] he analyzes the present political and economic order. To think about America in its contemporaneity is not only to try to grasp the injustices of its current political and economic system, but also those it has produced in the past. This Westian analysis is of the highest interest to those concerned with America's political and religious anthropology.

Not only does West show how the politico-religious alliance centered on economic interests sets up the system of domination, but he also exposes the mechanisms of reproduction. To achieve this, he analyzes the ritual logic of American institutions, because ritual logic is always the logic of creating and speaking beliefs and myths. Since rites allow for integration and control, their elucidation can effectively grasp strategies and mechanisms of domination.

Indeed, as Foucault would say, rites make it possible to monitor and punish. This economic-politico-religious surveillance takes place through language, rules, exchanges, and system of signs. In this sense, they are therefore a symbolic violence, that is, a violence that occurs on the mental structures of the concerned populations.

America has constructed its imaginary and symbolism from a cosmogony, an anthropology, and an ontology that are its own. To put it simply, America has elaborated

- its "cosmogony," or its vision of the world from a myth: the country of all opportunities, ideal island of human development;
- its "anthropology," or conception of social relations from violence; and
- its "ontology" or conception of what comprises the Being based on what the Being possesses.

Nihilists thus shape Americans' interpretive and evaluative patterns. West analyzes the elements coming from the registers of the imaginary, the real, and the symbolic to show how the American

---

[37] Cornel West, *Prophetic Reflections, Notes on Race and Power in America*, vol. 2 (Monroe, ME: Common Courage Press, 1993).

elite produces its discourse about itself and the rest of the world, and he denounces how this elite sets up special mechanisms for the victims to rehearse this discourse in unison. He concludes that everything is rigged.

According to him, it is from a hierarchy of legitimacy and a relationship of order based on having that these nihilists fashion what should be "an American's typical behavior," or even their being or citizenship. Therefore, to deconstruct these real mechanisms of domination that have often led to democratic failures and the reinforcement of injustices, we must go beyond the architectural structure of violence and nihilism. West suggests first tackling this domination's codes and symbolic structures that have been built throughout America's history. Thus, he analyzes in detail (notably in his book *Democracy Matters*) the links that unite the plutocrats with the political, economic, and even media and religious powers.

Combatant Solidarity

West asks himself, "Who has not felt overwhelmed by dread and despair when confronting the atrocities and barbarities of our world? And surely a cheap optimism or trite sentimentalism will not sustain us" (*Democracy Matters*, p. 216). He invites all those who love the spirit of justice and freedom to regroup: "When visionary and courageous citizens see through the dogmas and nihilisms of those who rule us and join together to pursue democratic individuality, progress can be made in our communities and our society" (*Democracy Matters*, p. 103).

The struggle to become aware of and denounce the system must occur first at the level of thought because the people often do not know how plutocrats transfer symbolic violence in the religious field, and vice versa. It must be shown that nihilism is spiritually empty and morally wrong. To do this, West proposes the use of Socratic questioning. He takes the example of Thrasymachus, who transposed into today's world incarnates of paternalistic and evangelical nihilism in West's view. This sophist argues with Socrates that force prevails over law: "Thrasymachus mocks truth, integrity, and principles by claiming that power, might, and force dictate desirable political action and public policy. Raw power rather than moral principles determines what is right. For him, the terms of what is just must be dictated by imperial elites because such exercise of power in necessary in order to ensure national security and prosperity" (*Democracy Matters*, p. 30).

But like any form of violence or nihilism, this control strategy can have an opposite effect to the desired one. It leads to the alienation of individual and collective freedom and pushes the masses to passivity: Everyone looks at each other and remains inactive. Individuals are designated specific positions for which they can best perform assigned tasks. To get them out of this, intellectuals and true leaders must join forces and support them effectively by proposing forms of organization that will enable them to carry out their individual praxis, that is, to offer them frameworks so that they can play an active role.

West says that Americans have been able to organize themselves to deal with injustices, especially when it comes to democracy. It is in the heart of imperial America that movements took root to defend some democratic ideals, although these movements were limited mainly to white citizens. "The formula of corporate elite power alongside racist division of the citizenry would seem to have prevailed, yet, fortunately, this formula often overreaches, resulting in corruption, graft, greed, internal bickering, and a democratic backlash" (*Democracy Matters*, p. 52).

In the face of the division of labor on the basis of ethnic and racial grounds, the people reacted with opposing democratic struggles. But these reactions failed to live up to expectations because the latent ideology that underpinned these struggles was segregation. The White elites who fought these battles believe they must preserve the racial position of Whites by insisting on difference, or even establishing differences with Blacks and Native peoples. From their viewpoint, segregation is a natural and legitimate standpoint. Moreover, with capitalism associating human value and market value, these elites, imbued with this ideology, consider that inequality between beings in general, and Blacks in particular, is a "natural" norm.

But though the justification matrix of the struggles led by these different movements is generally a segregationist and capitalist ideology, it is also framed by politico-religious safeguards. In other words, America is "God's chosen one," and it is to White men that God would have entrusted the mission of maintaining it. To grasp this Westian analysis of "democratic movements in America," let's take a close look at what comprises these movements.

Political and Trade Union Movements Between Democratic Radicalism and Segregation

Indeed, in the face of corrupt political and economic elites, major pro-democracy movements have emerged. But these movements have often been built on racial and identity bases. They are populist, progressive, and trade union movements.

> These movements did not question the racist, imperialist paradigm of the plutocrats and elites they challenged. Although the three forms of democratic radicalism initiated by white men in the American experience—populism, progressivism and trade unionism—contributed significantly to limiting the corruption and greed of plutocratic elites and corrupt politicians, they didn't take their demands all the way, for rarely did either movement target white supremacy or imperial expansion. (Democracy Matters, p. 52)

And for good reason: The populist movement led by farmers was a reaction to the market economy's fundamentalism, the kings of money and the "gilded age's business princes." These farmers wanted rural producers to have more democratic participation in government and economic policies.

As for the progressive movement, according to West, it was a reaction "an urban middle-class backlash against the corrupt ties of politicians to corporate elites and the unfettered greed of financial bosses" (*Democracy Matters*, p. 52). This movement wanted more democracy and bureaucratic efficiency in public policies.

Finally, with regard to the trade union movement led by the working class, often comprising new immigrants, it "was the worker-led backlash against the free-market fundamentalism of corporate owners and financial bosses. It called for more democratic control over the workplace, especially more say in wages paid to laborers" (*Democracy Matters*, p. 53).

These three movements were therefore not smitten with democratic spirit. Their leaders were xenophobic or even racist. West takes the example of Thomas Watson, president of the Populist Party in 1908, who, after struggling alongside Black farmers in the segregationist South, ended his career in the Ku Klux Klan. As for the progressives, its great representative, Woodrow Wilson, who would soon be elected president of the United States, reinstated racial segregation in Washington. His freedom charter in foreign policy did not take into account Asia, Latin America, or Africa. Finally, the great trade unionist Eugene Debs, who was president of the American Socialist Party, certainly led a crusade against the great disparities in wealth; nevertheless, despite his antiracist stance, he did not know how to, and could not integrate, people of color into the trade union movement.

The democratic struggles of these White leaders are not as democratic as they claim to be. "Most peoples of color were confined to poor rural communities, and wave after wave of immigration from Europe filled U.S. cities with a new population to be exploited as cheap laborers" (*Democracy Matters*, p. 52). The leaders of the populist, progressive, and trade union movements have never attacked the heart of the American political system: the exploitation of human beings and segregation. Therefore, according to West, the questions that should be asked are these: How have most of these American historical leaders been able to socially share and approve the assumptions and actions of the segregationist system? How could they legitimize the harmful excesses of the segregationist political and economic system, to the point that the system has become familiar and acceptable to many?

According to West, it is through a combination of religious and economic myths centered upon White supremacy that political leaders have inscribed their struggles. In complicity with some religious figures, especially Constantinian Christians, these politicians use subterfuge, not only to slip toward one to the other, but also to alienate the population.

On the one hand, it is the ability to possess material goods that determines citizenship status. On the other hand, with the complicity of some Christians, good citizenship is associated with Constantinian religious values. For this to work, ideological mechanisms centered upon property are established. But, more generally, for West, though in the past segregation was a form of radical extremism, it persists today through ultraliberal economic policies that choose to ignore society's structural problems, thereby participating in its dehumanization. This policy is deliberate.

Instead of organizing as a group in a spirit of solidarity, many citizens are "content to focus on private careers and be distracted with stimulating amusements. They have given up any real hope of shaping the collective destiny of the nation" (*Democracy Matters*, p. 27). Low-income people, especially African Americans, are assigned to an area of non-being, "arid drought," as Frantz Fanon would say. But West believes this zone can be "a launching pad" of new democratic possibilities from which the outcast's emancipation can be conceived.

Nihilism leads to the denial of all the moral and cultural values of minorities, and these voiceless groups try, as they have in the past, to find solutions through churches in order to live their solidarity, their existence, their humanity. But some of them are strongly pushed toward religious fanaticism, which blinds them and their understanding of the insidious mechanisms of domination slyly developed by the elite. These mechanisms of domination are seen less in the opposition between the democratic ideal and religious beliefs than in the expansion of materialism and false spiritualism.

These mechanisms of domination and these nihilistic strategies are dangerous even for those who implement them. In seeking to perpetuate conformism, they reinforce the status quo and therefore impede progress.

Struggles: Conceptual Mechanisms and Strategic Tools

Taking Du Bois's book *The Souls of Black Folk*, which deals with the African American identity, West addresses the issue of nihilism, leadership, and the struggle for emancipation. From the start of the twentieth century, Du Bois (1903) described the problem of "double consciousness" through the phenomenon of this invisible barrier of racial segregation that acts as a veil. He then showed that one perceives the other only through their own eyes and that "the other" represents one side of his or her own identity. We must lift the veils to see one other. Black Americans must accept their Africanity and their Americanity in order to reconcile their Black (African) side and their White (American) side.

Though Du Bois's analysis dates back to the beginning of the twentieth century, West points out that while the forms of assimilation have evolved and changed over the years, racial prejudice was not erased during the civil rights movement of the 1960s. In the confusion, with persistent pressure, the American normative culture has created an identity crisis that causes many Blacks to feel, as Du Bois remarks, "this sense of always looking at one's self through the eyes of others, of measuring one's soul by the tape of a world that looks on in amused contempt and pity."[38] This Duboisian analysis invites reflection on the question of the Being and existence.

Indeed, this issue of identity concerning Black Americans was analyzed by Du Bois and then by the authors of the Negritude movement to which Jean Paul Sartre was close. Renewing this debate today and recognizing the need for engagement, it seems important to read West using Sartre as a yardstick. West believes that this analysis needs to be updated to address the issue of identity. We will try to examine these Westian questions in light of the tools given by Sartre in *Being and Nothingness* (1943) and in *Critique of Dialectical Reason* (1960).

These two philosophers speak against a purely objective, purely social definition of the group. Both center their philosophies on identity, difference, and the universal and call for action and

---

[38] W.E.B. Du Bois, *The Souls of Black Folk*, (Chicago: A.C. McClurg & Co., 1903).

engagement. Should West qualify as Sartrean? The answer to this question can be found through several incursions into West's understanding of engagement.

CORNEL WEST, SARTREAN OR ANTI-SARTREAN POSTURE?

"Engagement," this Sartrean leitmotiv, is also West's creed. According to Sartre,

> The writer is situated in his time. Every word has consequences. Every silence, too. I hold Flaubert and Goncourt responsible for this repression which followed the Commune because they did not write one line to prevent it. One might say that it was not their business. But was the Calas trial Voltaire's business? Dreyfus' condemnation, Zola's? The administration of the Congo, Gide's? Each of these authors, in a special circumstance of his life, measures his responsibility as a writer. (*Les Temps Modernes*, No. 1)

Let us remember, West writes, "I do not want to be numbered among those who sold their souls for a mess of pottage—who surrendered their democratic Christian identity for a comfortable place at the table of the American empire while, like Lazarus, the least of these cried out and I was too intoxicated with worldly power and might to hear, beckon and heed their cries" (*Tragicomique Amérique*, p. 185).

Engagement is tied to the human condition: It takes constant engagement to be free. To engage oneself is to give one's self, and it is also to go toward others. Like Sartre, in *Being and Nothingness*, West considers that the relation to the Other is a constitutive fact of consciousness, but also in relation to this Other, we each must preserve our destiny's autonomy as much as we can. In the eyes of others, the individual refuses to be considered as a thing and avoids oscillating between the masochism through which one comes into being for the Other and the sadism which is the Other that comes into being for oneself.

For West, to engage is to grasp and tell the truth:

> A concrete expression of the truth of love happened to me during a field trip to an Indian reservation. I had never seen such abject poverty in the face of children. These red brothers and sisters were living in squalor. It was shocking and heartbreaking. Right then and there, I promised that I would never forget the suffering of indigenous people—I would never allow black suffering to blind me from the suffering of others, no matter what color, culture or civilization. I was saved from the mistake of devaluing other people's suffering. Later in life, I would never give a speech about the struggle for freedom without acknowledging the dignity and determination of Native American. (*Brother West: Living and Loving out Loud*, p. 50)

As we can see, for West, the motives for engagement may depend on local experiences or situations; however, they are relevant only if they are universal or can be universalized.

As is the case with Sartre, West always places the subject's absolute freedom at the center of human experience, and this freedom is a matter of strict individual consciousness. However, a collective project becomes necessary so that the freedom of the Other does not dissolve into my being and my freedom is also not denied by that of the Other. But what are the conditions and possibilities of this collective project? How can people, passively assembled in impotence and separation by American institutions, suddenly be able to bring about an active unity in which they can acknowledge one other? To better grasp the Sartrean dread in West's work, let's take a detour to what Sartre thought about individuals waiting for a bus.

According to Sartre, at a bus stop, when the bus does not arrive, there is initially a passive indifference: the series, a passive unit of the masses. The series is therefore a collective form of social inertia. At a certain point, some people will protest and murmur. This is the group in formation. The wait is prolonged, and the subjects are led to talk to each other. The group is formed.

At this stage of the group's formation, an element of fusion appears: The individuals address each other because they find the wait unbearable. "The other is the same as I and not my other."[39] When the group gets organized, the same is everywhere; we are in a merged group. Each member manifests to the other that everyone is united around the same cause.

Thus, if an individual without institutional status starts the protest, everyone follows. Whoever starts, followed by others in this protest, is a third-party regulator, since it is the link between the other and me, says Sartre. How is this Sartrean approach to historical movements supported in Westian philosophy?

Using Sartrean tools to analyze the effects of Black leaders' nihilism in their community, West shows how we end up with the series, or the passive unity of the masses. To combat nihilism, it is imperative to simultaneously organize and carry out individual and collective actions because, despite nihilism's unitary form, it must be remembered that nihilism comes in multiple forms. It is important to unmask it wherever it appears.

West shows that the Black civic movement was built in opposition to the series by a unifying revolt that resulted in a sense of brother- and sisterhood. But the way it has been institutionalized pushes some Black leaders to implement policies of terror. This could explain the return to the series, the passivity of Black populations.

To better understand the parallel that we make of Sartrean and Westian analyses, let us revisit a stage in recent African American history. Take the case of the Montgomery bus protest, when Black Americans revolted by the inhumanity of Jim Crow decided that "the wait" was unbearable. This sequence of protests,[40] triggered by Rosa Parks, allowed Blacks to go beyond the series, but also to

---

[39] Jean Paul Sartre, *Critique de la Raison Dialectique* (Ibidem).
[40] In Montgomery, Alabama, while Jim Crow forbade Black people to sit at the front of buses, Rosa Parks, a young Black woman, decided one day to take a seat in this forbidden part of the bus. After this incident, Blacks decided to organize the Montgomery bus boycott.

form a merged group in which each actor seemed to play the role of third-party regulator. Subsequently, to avoid dispersal, every member of the Black civil rights movement swore allegiance to the group and its founders, such as Martin Luther King Jr.

It must be said that large institutional figures such as King have ensured the longevity of the Black civil rights movement. The implicit or explicit oath of its activists and militants have allowed the movement to continue until the death of the great Black leader. Although this movement still exists, after the death of Dr. King, several movements took root. But why did we move from a merged group to movement, to institution, and to the series?

Before responding to this question as Sartre did, let us say with West that, certainly, all the leaders of these movements invoke fraternity, but very often, many use it as trap to enlist members and control them in order to get rich on their backs. They easily succeed in doing so as the wounds that are at the origin of the Black struggle persist.

These African American leaders do not respect the mutual aid obligations that are the foundation of civic movements. Among these Black elite, terror[41] prevails over fraternity (*Race Matters*, 1993). These leaders, who are very often men of the Church, create divisions by legitimizing their organizations and their economic actions through religion in order to better exercise their domination. Some of them, like lobbying groups in American society, institute terror to satisfy their interests. Thus, some do not hesitate to ask their often-faithful members for large sums of money.

Indeed, knowing the importance of religious faith in African American populations, some leaders do not refrain from asking their members to swear an oath. This alienation strategy doesn't only affect isolated individuals. It makes it possible to group all individuals into a single "body," which is both social and religious. By prescribing the possibility of punishment by the group or by

---

[41] See, for instance, the Terror under Robespierre during the French Revolution.

ACTIVISM AND THE POETICS OF COMMITMENT 133

God, the oath instills terror not only in the individual but also in the whole group. Thus, through the fact that each member of these groups is afraid of being considered a traitor, the group establishes a terrorist reciprocity within itself.

Unfortunately, by introducing terror, these nihilist leaders bring people back to the starting point: the serial collective. Nobody can criticize these nihilist leaders and their actions. What's worse, often each member feels as though they are being watched and is therefore wary of the other. In a climate of terror, the group's fusion is lost.

It seems that this climate of terror is the reason for West's reluctance to fully engage as an active member in some civil rights organizations. This may also be the reason King did not have any official institutional status. However, when Dr. King began to get involved in protests, millions of citizens followed suit, which made him the leader and guide of this protest group. Certainly, his religious faith served as a guarantee to the other members of the group, assuring them that he would not betray their common cause. King, however, never invoked or imposed the Christian faith as a prerequisite for membership in the civil rights movement. It should be remembered that most African American organizations are affiliated with religion. And very often, religion encourages or institutes the oath as a pledge of fidelity. The oath is sacred in religions. Let us emphasize, like Sartre, the oath leads to freedom and terror at the same time. It is at the beginning of human relations and at the end of the merged group. At the same time, it is an indispensable guarantee against tyranny since it allows the group to form and resist. It is also a means of instilling terror, with everyone fearing being perceived as a traitor. The oath is therefore a source of fraternity/terror. How, then, can the oath save the group from social inertia and produce an active unity?

We will not discuss in detail here the philosophical questions to which the oath returns us. We are just going to argue how the internalized sacred figure, like that of King, by African Americans, has helped them in their struggles for freedom.

For Sartre, the sacred is the fundamental structure of terror. For example, a king's coronation is nothing other than the transcendence of the king's power. In other words, the coronation means that the king's power comes from God. From this point of view, the religiously sacred can justify tyranny.

The transcendence of religion can only produce a serial unity. By its definition, the sacred denies other possibilities that do not fit within its framework. The oath therefore has a negative relation to freedoms. In the same way, the oath that makes it possible to commit oneself to the future is, according to Sartre, impossible unless one is acting bad faith because I am only what I do and I do not presently know what my project will be under penalty of chaining my freedom. For Sartre, it is useless to swear an oath in the present if we know that nothing can bind us in the future.

West says he lives with fear and anxiety, with the absurdity of the human condition, through the prism of the cross. Christ's cross or the sacred figure of King allows him to demonstrate that the oath can be an energy for freedom, for though the oath is transcendence toward the future, it is also a means through which African Americans emphasize their fidelity to sacred historical figures. We see here that the oath touches upon the question of tension vis-à-vis transcendence—immanence. In these conditions, how does one escape terror/fraternity? How do we get rid of what can be considered the metaphysics of collective salvation suggested by the oath, as a guarantee for the group? Moreover, how can one escape from the metaphysics of individual salvation (of individual salvation) suggested by the American capitalist system?

Very often, West replies that he manages to escape the dictatorship of the collective and individualism by finding his inspiration on two levels: the philosophical and the religious. On the philosophical level, it is Socratic love, especially through *paideia*,[42] an educational method for self-elevation, that enables him to engage his own history, his memory, and his morality with love and criticism. West often uses the word *paideia* to talk about deep education that

---

[42] *Paidea* is a Greek word that means raising.

allows for the serious consideration of existential problems (*Brother West: Living and Loving out Loud*, p. 22). According to West, this paideia is on the religious plane of Christian prophetic inspiration, especially of the Baptist church embodied by King. He writes that, like King, he tries to be a prisoner of hope, a fanatic of fairness and justice, and an extremist of love.

Method: Philosophical Gesture and Prophetic Impetus

For West, individual and collective salvation can come through religion, because to be a Christian and a follower of Christ is to love wisdom. Therefore, both prophetic Christianity and philosophy lead to the love of wisdom. Thus, he thinks that the oath of religious prophecy does not lead to the series but rather encourages dynamism. Let us recall that the series is the situation in which individuals are passive, but religious prophecy invites us to be active in the search for peace, justice, and love. Even though lobbying groups constantly disrupt organizations to render them fragmented series, religious prophecy helps to strengthen and maintain fraternity.

Prophetic witness contains Socratic questioning and tragicomic hope. It is radical love in Christian freedom and radical freedom in Christian love. Unlike Sartrean seriality, West turns to prophecy, African American art, and the search for the Being's significance in society. As we have seen, the places where we find groups and series are also privileged places to reflect on the Being and existence, places where we can grasp the tension between immanence and transcendence.

Similarly, art is a place to reflect on the role of intermediation because artists, in their groups, are third-party regulators without privileged status, and their commitment comes only from their sovereign decision. But, very often, thanks to religious prophecy, they not only dissolve the series, but also unify the movement. Relying on religious prophecy to commit to God allows the group to avoid the risk of being dispersed in relation to the ideal.

What is interesting in West's conceptual tooling is not only the appropriation of a deconstruction method with respect to nihilism in the civil rights movement, but also the highlighting of a system of analysis of the motives of engagement. In a more global approach, West attacks the intellectual and religious citadels that smolder and coat the plutocrats and gravediggers of democracy. He sifts through political language and religious language, as well as their connections, to show that the American elite build themselves and their general discourse on lies and omissions. He also reveals how this politico-religious ideology, founded on new forms of violence, not only alienates populations, but also erodes democracy. He calls, therefore, for an energetic fight against the perversion of the democratic system. This fight also opposes neoliberalism and American imperialism. Certainly, he says, here and there, there are social and political forms of resistance, but many are limited to minor reforms.

However, we must profoundly change the system and avoid falling into the system of stultification implemented by the elite. He invites his fellow citizens to engage in political struggles and to deconstruct the psychic mechanisms of domination that are mainly rooted in Constantinian Christianity's politico-religious discourse. But from these gaps, voids, and holes to which the imperialist and materialist actions and ideals of the political-religious alliance lead us, he wants us to create an opportunity to reformulate and develop renewed thinking with regard to citizenship and emancipation. He invites us to use what he calls the blues model and the prophetic Christianity model to deconstruct prejudices.

In other words, West believes that marginalized places are places where all of society can untie the knots of nihilism. Thus, art and culture appear to him as the means of building a harmonious life. These are places where we can save all of America that is aboard the same ship pitching in oceans of misery. Art makes it possible to cast off the moorings, to tell the truth and take a new direction.

On the whole, West's engagement is characterized by his refusal to abdicate before any form of individualistic or collective oppression. He carries out his activism in societal life while showing the dangers of indoctrination. He is aware that actually engaging in a group's action for a cause can lead to misunderstandings or suspicions on the part of adversaries.

This risk is all the greater because he does not limit his involvement to the academic world; he also forges alliances with marginalized, artists, the "voiceless," the low income, and the outcast. He has taught in prisons for twenty-three years, and he often participates in social movements such as Occupy Wall Street, or the march for Ferguson. In *Democracy Matters*, he ponders, "Who has not felt overwhelmed by dread and despair when confronting the atrocities and barbarities of our world? And surely cheap optimism and trite sentimentality will not sustain us. We need a bloodstained Socratic love and tear-soaked prophetic love fueled by a hard-won tragicomic hope" (p. 156).

DISSONANCE

West's thought presents another approach and invites the use of new investigative methods. West inscribes prophecy in the field of philosophy and uses African American art to philosophize. By engaging in the collective on the one hand and using religion and art to philosophize on the other, he confirms to us that philosophy is not itself a producer of truths. It seizes them where they are. By forging his ethics from African American culture and academic and religious teachings, West invests in, until recently, barely explored fields to show us that there are other places and temporalities to think about life and access the Being. He carries out this work in the subjective American world, constantly confronting most of the elite's ethics with his own.

This confrontation is based on a dialectical work of the visible and the invisible, on hermeneutics (the art of interpreting images) and semiotics (the analysis of the production and reception of speech). He appropriates this *contretemps* not only to show the differences between his temporality and that of the American elite, but also to highlight the difference between the outcast and the leaders. This is an original approach that permits starting from experimental practices to think about or consolidate democracy. But these differences in temporality do not exclude the possibility of agreement. West insists that the prophetic word of the bluesman and the rapper invites dialogue.

While each of these categories uses language to distinguish themselves, all of them show that even when marginalized in the capitalist system, we can contribute to building a better world. The essential thing is having the will to transgress borders, be they political, religious, or racial. To engage is to try to set up a chain of solidarity among all people concerned with equality and justice. But to engage is also to seek solutions to collective problems. West believes that African American art offers enormous possibilities for conflict resolution.

It is not a question of fetishizing the music, but of making it a vibrant hearth that forges bonds: the object (music) comes from the self and is transferred to the Other. Thus, African American music—jazz, blues, and soul—will contribute to the peaceful and harmonious presence of America in the world, and the world in America. Through his analysis of the blues, his philosophy, and his poetics of commitment, West strives at the same time to comply with and then escape prescribed standards.

African American music, especially jazz and blues, allows you to forge ahead, to draw lines of progress and carve out spaces of freedom, which can be used to get along and build a harmonious society. According to West, African American art is one of the privileged ways to engage in politics, to emancipate oneself.

8
CORNEL WEST: A FIGURE WORTH FOLLOWING

Throughout this book, we have shown that West is an enigmatic and atypical figure in American intellectual life. Contrary to American analytic philosophy, which is dominated essentially by logic, he perpetuates European "continental" philosophy that is geared toward exegesis and history. He takes the necessary distance to analyze the troubles and turmoil of social life. He tries to seize the breath of outcast peoples like someone who is scaling volcanic mountains, carrying the weight of history on his back. At the summit, he embodies the soul of the volcano in order to feel it better and take action.

Yet in a country where race matters, isn't having such an attitude not only risking not being loved by some, but also being strongly hated by others? For West, the search for truth and justice is worth every engagement. To seek justice is to try to grasp the path of truth in all the components of society.

Thus, he plunges into the troubled waters of religion and art to elaborate philosophical thought. He questions the role and place of individuals and social bodies, images, sounds, the flow of objects, intermediation, and solidarity, all in order to think about conditions for harmoniously living together. He immerses himself in the culture of chocolate cities, these places and spaces in turbulence, agitation, disorder, animation, dissipation, vivacity, impetuous whirlwinds, to grasp the components of misunderstanding. From these spaces in turbulence, he shows us that the conditions of misunderstanding are to be found in institutions and in the elements that structure mentalities such as White supremacist ideology.

There are some individuals who resist this supremacist ideology that is sometimes internalized by minority groups. And West points out that these forms of resistance can only be grasped in their meanings when we take into account other social structures internalized by these populations. In fact, these populations, which are often excluded from the dominant economic and political systems, will invest in the exclusion zones in order to give meaning to their lives. They will try to develop strategies for survival and for the recognition of their identity. Music, performances, sports, and the Church serve as places of humanity, expressions of talent, and corporal and spiritual know-how.

Although excluded peoples are propelled by American capitalism, which leads them to radical alterity, they face this test of isolation as an opportunity to invent and renew themselves in the social, artistic, and cultural fields. The realizations of these populations are made possible, channeled, displaced, repaired, refined, sublimated, reinforced, and played out with potentially infinite resources and combinations of their symbolic systems. The restoring efforts for recognition carried out by these populations whose lives are fragmented cannot be understood outside of the history of African American culture.

The importance that individuals and groups attach to their cultural values escapes many intellectuals all the time. Hence the questions that could be asked of West is this: Are symbolism and realities experienced by populations fundamental in rethinking justice? Are interactions between the intelligentsia and the working classes necessary for social transformation?

For West, if the task of philosophers is to think about the conditions of possibilities of justice, they must be full of collective experiences. But he adds that this approach must be accompanied by a critical approach, for it is critical reasoning based on philosophical humility, intellectual integrity, and personal sincerity that will make it possible to fight against the corruption of the elites (*Tragicomique Amérique*, p. 223).

Philosophers must have the courage to show the mechanisms of the American capitalist system's self-legitimization that hinder the development of justice; they have to show the links between the "horror" of slavery and the ruins of American capitalism. They must also have the courage to evaluate the gaps between the principles of equality, justice, and freedom in relation to social realities.

Beyond the great principles enunciated by the American elites, West denounces forms of violence and nihilism. The structure of violence and paternalistic, evangelical, or sentimental nihilism that are exerted on low-income populations in America should be pointed out. The intellectual has the duty to deconstruct ambiguity, which has allowed plutocrats to dig trenches around democracy within and outside of the US. There is an alliance between American and foreign plutocrats that annihilates any possibility of developing national and international justice. This class of national and international plutocrats seeks, by all means, to hide the capitalist system's contradictions and misdeeds, all the more so because these internal forms of violence are translated into aggressive foreign policies, preemptive invasions, and wars.

According to West, plutocrats' and politicians' rhetoric makes people believe that the American political and economic systems are the best in the world. These plutocrats and politicians put in place strategies of domination, which, despite marked opposition, are shared by the majority of Americans. The latter are often persuaded that "American values" are the best in the world, and therefore must be shared by the rest of the world. Moreover, it is these values that distinguish them from the rest of the world. This belief is so strong that many minorities in America are persuaded that no system is viable apart from the US model. By internalizing and reproducing these allegedly universal values, these minorities renew the forms of injustice in their communities. We must therefore deconstruct the systems of evaluating, classifying, and ranking capitalism.

It should also be emphasized that this so-called consciousness and responsibility of America to be the most democratically evolved of democracy, for democracy is never fully achieved or complete.

Including America itself, one can notice that there is a portion of the citizenry who are excluded by the political system.

In other words, by plunging into the chocolate cities and vanilla suburbs, the American intellectual can employ a dialectical method, to show the gaps in the formation of this collective consciousness. Of course, West acknowledges that some intellectuals have deconstructed the psychic mechanisms of domination, stultification, and nihilism implemented by the elite, but very often the resistance of many social movements and trade unions are limited to promoting small reforms that fail to contain the constant social crises.

To overcome the social crises that drive the whole nation into emptiness, into a ditch, and make it go around in circles, he suggests becoming more aware of the system's defects and limitations—in order to reformulate and develop renewed ways of thinking about citizenship and emancipation. For West, this means that everyone must engage in the struggles of social and civic movements. That said, he stresses that social and civic movements can also be sources of alienation.

West purports that the best way to free oneself from the metaphysics of individual salvation suggested by capitalism, to tear oneself away from the metaphysics of collective salvation suggested by the dynamics of the masses, is to be inspired by the world of art and prophetic religion.

In America, where religion and capitalism are so present, if we want to fight against the elements that challenge the values of Beings and destabilize the collective, prophetic Christianity and African American musical forms are the means to combat all forms of alienation and to consolidate social ties and democracy. Thus, contrary to Constantinian Christianity allied with the political powers that alienate individuals, prophetic Christianity liberates them. Like the musicians in the jazz and blues bands, music impregnated with prophecy allows everyone to affirm their freedom and express their truth. Prophetic Christianity and African American art make it possible to escape all forms of oppression, whether individualist or collective. Indeed, prophetic Christianity, and art in general, blues in particular, call for freedom, love, and justice.

Instead of seeking to deny the other or to be denied by the other, the bluesman and the jazzman, in a conscious momentum of the relation to the Other, invite the cultivation of love. It is love and communion that will help to avoid the nihilism and violence facing America and all humanity. African American musicians are the guardians of the temple. They seek to transform tragedy into hope—hence the Westian concept of the tragicomic—and escape from the cycle of vengeance. Thus, after the heinous and inhumane terrorist attacks on America, on September 11, 2001, West said that it is necessary to vigorously condemn and fight against all forms of terrorism, but America must not enter a cycle of violence and revenge.

It is the whole American nation that has been neglected; it has experienced what it is to be Black in America. On that day, the whole of America was subjected to the test of gratuitous violence and experienced what it is like to live in insecurity. A few days after this attack, the whole nation had the blues. West invited the blues nation to draw inspiration from the blues people: It is the blues that will allow America to emerge from its blues.

Living in permanent insecurity, Blacks, instead of letting themselves be slaughtered, were able to cure themselves of their deep sadness caused by racist terror. Afro-Americans, victims of White supremacist terrorism, have strengthened themselves spiritually and culturally, to resist socially, physically, and emotionally, by singing the blues. If the blues is a state, an experienced emotion lived, it is also, let us repeat, a language of exit from crisis.

The epistemological interest of West's analysis in the field of music allows us to work within domains that appear antithetical: secularity and religion, difference and identity, multiple and universal, fragmentation and summation. These areas analyzed by West refer to essential questions in philosophy, which converge with a general anthropology, thereby contributing to defining the structural elements of social actions and policies geared toward the politics of the "invisible," marginalized populations.

Similarly, West's analysis of African Americans' cultural reproductions sheds light on the notions of game sense, practical sense, strategy, and distinction. More generally, starting from the axiom that, like every being, African Americans internalize the societal structure and themselves become the objective structure of the historical-cultural world, West gives sociologists interesting material to understand African American behaviors and practices. In other words, it is impossible to study African American social, cultural, and economic practices without taking into account their interactions with other segments of American society and weighing African American history. However, one should not limit oneself in Manichaeism.

In sum, on a kind of swing, West's work invites us to rid ourselves of ideological constraints. We oscillate between singularity and plurality, between the here and there, and the near and the far.

POST SCRIPTUM

In the intricate tapestry of intellectual thought and cultural identity, West emerges as a figure whose journey is marked by a profound engagement with a diverse array of philosophical, literary, and ethical influences. Rooted in the traumatic experiences of his African American community, his intellectual pursuits are a testament to the complex interplay between personal history and global philosophical currents.

West's exploration of the African American experience is deeply influenced by the works of prominent thinkers such as Du Bois, Richard Wright, James Baldwin, and Toni Morrison. Through their lenses, he interprets the struggles and resilience of his community, creating a rich narrative that shapes his intellectual identity.

In grappling with the absurdity of the human condition, West delves into the teachings of Søren Kierkegaard, Anton Chekhov, and a multitude of global intellectuals. Kierkegaard's approach to combating the inherent melancholy and sadness in human existence resonates profoundly with West, inspiring him to forge a profound link between the quest for meaning and the pursuit of freedom.

The quest for liberation, however, extends beyond Kierkegaard. West draws inspiration from Chekhov and other global intellectuals, seeing in them beacons of love, empathy, and devotion to others. In the face of the tragicomic human predicament, he views these figures as champions of values that defy market logic and elevate humanity above the mundane.

Samuel Beckett becomes another compass in West's intellectual journey, as he explores the abyss of despair, nostalgia, hope, and the complex relationship with time. Literature and philosophy serve as West's tools to capture the intricacies of the human experience and the ways individuals cope with existential challenges.

The exploration of Arthur Schopenhauer's writings adds another layer to West's intellectual tapestry. Delving into themes of sadness, sorrow, compassion, and justice, he seeks to enrich his understanding and contribute to a nuanced comprehension of the human condition.

West's commitment to publishing two articles and a book this year reflects not only his dedication to academic excellence but also his tireless quest for meaning and justice. His writing, deeply rooted in African American culture and the world of music, weaves together various philosophical currents, from Marxism to pragmatism and radical humanism.

The influence of W.E.B. Du Bois is pivotal in West's pursuit of justice and equality. Du Bois's work serves as a guiding force, offering insights into the history of the Civil War, racial segregation, and the persistent racism that continues to plague American society.

West's engagement with Marxism, while critical, is rooted in a broader perspective that goes beyond the classical interpretations of Marx and Engels. He recognizes the role of religion as a form of protest against social injustice within the Marxist framework, enriching his understanding of this complex ideology.

The integration of blues into various aspects of life, including religion, intellect, and politics, underscores West's commitment to addressing the tragedies in African American history. The blues, for him, becomes a resilient melody that fights against melancholy and darkness, affirming the human spirit in the face of adversity.

As a "blues-infected philosopher," West's engagement with Marx's critical thinking takes a unique trajectory. He extracts ethical dimensions crucial to understanding the human condition and bridges Marxism with Martin Luther King Jr.'s prophetic Christianity, creating a synthesis of political philosophy and ethical values.

The early intellectual influences on West, from Lukacs to Hegel, lay the groundwork for his later contributions. His exploration of Marxism goes beyond the traditional boundaries, emphasizing the importance of historical writings and the religious dimension within Marxist thought.

West's prophetic pragmatism, a term coined to describe his approach, draws on a diverse range of philosophical currents, from classical American pragmatism to neo-pragmatism. John Dewey's emphasis on education and democracy becomes a cornerstone, aligning with West's vision of fostering coexistence and democratic vitality.

The neo-Gramscian pragmatist perspective further refines West's approach, distinguishing between "organic" and "traditional" intellectuals. The organic intellectual, deeply connected to prophetic movements, considers the living conditions of ordinary people in their intellectual pursuits.

Rorty's neo-pragmatism challenges traditional philosophical discourse, emphasizing the importance of creating conditions for a better future rather than adhering to a utopian ideal. This resonates with West's commitment to solidarity over the pursuit of objectivity and truth.

In navigating the complexities of cultural identity and existence, West's engagement with Sartre provides a nuanced exploration. While sharing certain similarities, West diverges from Sartre in his emphasis on solidarity, community, and the spiritual dimension. The term *Sartrean* may capture a facet of his philosophy, but West's unique blend of influences requires a more nuanced classification.

In essence, West's intellectual journey is a testament to the richness that emerges from the interplay of diverse influences. From the blues-infused exploration of African American history to the nuanced engagement with philosophical currents, West's holistic approach contributes to a vision of a more equitable and united world. His commitment to justice, equality, and the relentless pursuit of meaning resonates through the intricate threads of his intellectual tapestry, creating a narrative that transcends boundaries and enriches our understanding of the human experience.

ACKNOWLEDGMENTS

To Professors Kwame Anthony Appiah (NYU), Souleymane Bachir Diagne (Columbia University), Stéphane Douailler (Paris St. Denis–Sorbonne), Henry Louis Gates, Jr. (Harvard University), Simon Gikandi (Princeton University),

To writers and artists: Late Manu Dibango (musician, Cameroun/France), Gael Faye (musician and writer, Rwanda/France), Cheikh Hamidou Kane (writer, Senegal).

SPECIAL THANKS

To Arlette for her corrections, suggestions, and for having helped me to better translate and formulate my thinking,

To Heather Lord, for her critiques, edits, suggestions, and insights,

To Emilienne Akpan, Gina Ba, Joel Dreyfus, Alexandra Mzuhali, Medina Niang, for their review.

My gratitude to friends, because of whom I was able to realize this book in peace:

Christophe Amiel, Amadou Mahtar Ba, Mohamed Camara, Ely Dieng, Alain Malick Diop, Nicolas Janin, Momar Mbengue, Cheikh Mboup, Oumar Seck, Pap Ngom.

They wrote the following about the book:

"Cornel West has had an extraordinary impact in American thought. This translation will help English-speaking readers to understand his impact beyond our shores."

Kwame Anthony Appiah, Professor, New York University

"Mahamadou Lamine Sagna rightly emphasizes the importance of Socrates' philosophy in the thought of Cornel West. More than a Socratic way of thinking, he adds, West manifests a "Socratic posture," the very position the philosopher held *in the face of Athens* and injustice, but also *in the name of Athens* and what it ought to be. Defiance? No: love. For Socrates as for West, standing for justice is always in the name of a politics of love. Because for West, love, as Sagna demonstrates, is fundamental for society. By putting at the center of his "Rebellious Thoughts" the religion of love Mahamadou Lamine Sagna has well served the philosophy of Cornel West. And done immense service to all of us."

Souleymane Bachir Diagne, Professor, Columbia University

"For years, Mahamadou Lamine Sagna has retreated to solitary spaces where he has dedicated himself to writing a book, only emerging periodically as an unwavering supporter and facilitator of collective engagement in the inventive transformation of our societies. This book focuses entirely on the American Philosopher Cornel West, and Sagna's aim is to pass it on to us. It is a very old gesture that Mahamadou Lamine Sagna revives for us and with regard to Cornel West by telling us: Tolle, lege!—take it, and read it!"

Stéphane Douailler, Professor Emeritus, Paris University

"Certainly, comparison is not right, but by an extraordinary convergence the sociologist Mahamadou Lamine Sagna's essay on Cornel West illuminates my own writing or filmed biographies: The jazz infected and Blues saturated philosopher, Cornel West, is soaked in Makossa!"

Manu Dibango, Musician, Cameroon/France

"From the chains of slavery to gold chains, from cotton fields to the songs of concrete, from blues to rap, this book by Mamadou Lamine Sagna shows that America's greatest invention is and will remain popular music."

Gael Faye, Author/Rapper, France/Rwanda

"In this undulating, poignant and joyful book, the Senegalese/French sociologist Mahamadou Lamine Sagna shows us how Cornel West illuminates obscurantism and contributes to transmit the torch of knowledge from generation to generation. Cornel West is that rarest of contemporary philosophers, combining the breadth and depth of the broadly read, deeply comprehensive scholar with the range and reach of a great public intellectual, in a Harvard tradition that commenced perhaps with Emerson (Class of 1821) and Thoreau (Class of 1837), extending to William James (MD, 1869) and W.E.B. Du Bois (Class of 1890, PhD 1985). West is the brilliant, living embodiment of this great tradition in the American academy, possessing not only a truly original mind but also a *sui generis* manner of expressing that mind. One experiences the expression of his wisdom, and the nuances of his thinking, with awe."

Henry Louis Gates, Jr., Professor, Harvard University

"In this book, Mahamadou Lamine Sagna brings new insights into the writings and reflections of Cornel West, the distinguished American philosopher and public intellectual, showing us how his work matters especially in an age when race and violence have come to define modern life. Here we have not only a portrait of Cornel West as a man of faith, but also as a scholar and activist, one who is able to be at home both in the seminar room and the streets. A major achievement of this book is Sagna's ability to interpret West's philosophy and activism together as part of a larger meditation on race and suffering and the continuous search for a humanism yet to come."

Simon Gikandi, Professor, Princeton University

"The brilliant Senegalese sociologist and intellectual Mahamadou Lamine Sagna shows us how his colleague and friend Cornel West, "Master Griot" of modern times, forges a Miraculous Arms for the conquest of a truly universal postmodernity. From a fascinating portrait of this philosopher who uses the philosophical, traditional, religious, and artistic Afro-American patrimonies to deconstruct violence *and* nihilism in American political system, ML Sagna gives us new avenues to analyze the "Modernity's Ambiguity.""

Cheikh Hamidou Kane, Writer, Senegal

REFERENCES

KEY WORKS OF CORNEL WEST

West, Cornel. 1982. *Prophecy Deliverance! An Afro-American Revolutionary Christianity*. Philadelphia: The Westminster Press.

———. 1983. *The Prophetic Role of Churches*. Paris: Le Monde Diplomatique.

———. 1988. *Prophetic Fragments*. Trenton, NJ: Africa World Press.

———. 1989. *The American Evasion of Philosophy*. Madison: University of Wisconsin Press.

———. 1991. *The Ethical Dimensions of Marxist Thought*. New York: Monthly Review Press.

———. 1993. *Beyond Eurocentrism and Multiculturalism; Prophetic Thought in Postmodern Times*, vol. 1. Monroe ME: Common Courage Press.

———. 1993. *Keeping Faith: Philosophy and Race in America*. New York: Routledge.

———. 1993. *Prophetic Reflections: Notes on Race and Power in America*. Monroe, ME: Common Courage Press.

———. 1993. *Race Matters*. Boston: Beacon Press.

———. 1999. *Restoring Hope*. Boston: Beacon Press.

———. 1999. *The Cornel West Reader*. New York: Basic Books.

———. 2004. *Democracy Matters*. New York: Penguin.

———. 2005. *Tragicomique Amérique*. Paris: Payot.

———. 2008. *Hope on a Tightrope: Words and Wisdom*. 1st ed. New York: Smiley Books.

———. 2010. *Brother West: Living and Loving Out Loud. A Memoir*. 2nd ed. New York: Smiley Books.

West, Cornel, and Eddie S. J. Glaude. 2004. *African American Religious Thought: An Anthology*. Louisville, KY: Westminster John Knox Press.

West, Cornel, and Henry Louis J. Gates. 1996. *The Future of the Race*. New York: Vintage.

———. 2000. *The African-American Century*. New York: The Free Press.

———. 2000. *The African-American Century: How Black Americans Have Shaped Our Century*. New York: Simon and Schuster.

West, Cornel, and Sylvia Ann Hewlett. 1998. *The War Against Parents*. Boston: Houghton Mifflin.

West, Cornel, and bell hooks. 1991. *Breaking Bread*. Boston: South End Press.

West, Cornel, and Michael Lerner. 1995. *Jews and Blacks: Let the Healing Begin*. New York: Putnam.

West, Cornel, and Michael Lerner. 1996. *Jews and Blacks: A Dialogue on Race, Religion, and Culture in America*. New York: Dutton/Plume.

West, Cornel, and John Rajchman. 1985. *Post-Analytic Philosophy*. New York: Columbia University Press.

West, Cornel, and Roberto Mangabeira Unger. 1999. *The Future of American Progressivism*. Boston: Beacon Press.

West, Cornel, et al. 1990. *Out There: Marginalization and Contemporary Cultures*. Boston: MIT Press.

West, Cornel, Kara Keeling, and Colin McCabe, Eds. 2003. *Racist Traces and Other Writings: European Pedigrees/African Contagions* by James A. Snead. New York: Palgrave Macmillan.

West, Cornel, and John Rajchman. 1991. *La pensée américaine contemporaine*. Traduit en français par Andrée Lyotard sous le titre. Préface de Jean-François Lyotard. Paris: Presses universitaires de France.

OTHER REFERENCES

Anderson, Elizabeth. 2005. Dewey's Moral Philosophy. In *Stanford Encyclopedia of Philosophy*.
Badiou, Alain. 1992. *Conditions*. Paris: Éditions du Seuil.
Badiou, Alain. 2008. *Petit Panthéon Portatif*. Paris: La Fabrique Éditions.
Baldwin, James. 1996. *La prochaine fois, le feu*. Paris: Gallimard.
Baraka, Amiri. 1999. *Blues People: Negro Music in White America*. New York: Harper Perennial.
Barthes, Roland. 1993. *Œuvres complètes de Roland Barthes*, Tome 1. Paris: Seuil.
Baudelaire, Charles. 2010. *Le peintre de la vie moderne*. Paris: Fayard/Mille et une nuits.
Boulad-Ayoub, Josiane. 1995. *Mimes et parades: L'activité symbolique dans la vie sociale*. Paris: L'Harmattan.
Brent, Joseph. 1998. *Charles Sanders Peirce: A life, 2nd Edition*. Bloomington: Indiana University Press.
Chomsky, Noam. 1965. *Aspects of the Theory of Syntax*. Special ed. Cambridge: MIT Press.
Deleuze, Gilles. 1969. *Logique du sens*. Paris: Les Editions de Minuit.
Dixie, Quinton Hosford, and West, Cornel, Eds. 1999. *The Courage to Hope: From Black Suffering to Human Redemption*. Boston: Beacon Press.
Du Bois, W. E. B. 1903. *The Souls of Black Folks*. Chicago: A.C. Clurg and Co.
Ellison, Ralph Waldo 1952. *Invisible Man*. New York: Random House.
Foucault, Michel. 1969. *Archéologie du Savoir*. Paris: Gallimard.
Maximin, Daniel. 2013. *Aimé Césaire, Frère Volcan*. Paris: Éditions du Seuil.
Morrison, Toni. 2008. *Beloved*. Paris: Éditions 10x18.
Niane, Djibril Tamsir. 1960. *Soundjata ou l'épopée mandingue*. Paris: Présence Africaine.
Rancière, Jacques. 1995. *La mésentente*. Paris: Galilée.
———. 1998. *Aux bords du Politique*. Paris: Gallimard.
———. (2010). *Le Spectateur Emancipé*. Paris: La Fabrique.

Revue, L. (No 1). *Les Temps modernes.*
Sartre, Jean Paul. 1943. *Being and Nothingness.* New York: Washington Square Press.
———. 1960. *Critique of Dialectical Reason.* Paris: Gallimard.
———. 1960. *Critique de la Raison Dialectique.* Paris: Gallimard.
Wright, Richard. 1988. *L'enfant du pas (Native Son).* Paris: Gallimard.

USEFUL LINKS

http://www.pragmatism.org/library/west/index.htm
http://www.cornelwest.com/

INDEX

A

Abeles, Marc, 10, 26
Abid al-Jabri, Mohamed, 39
Abraham, 32, 35
Aesthetic, 9, 75, 86–87, 95, 97, 107
Affirmative action, 22, 62, 106
Afrika Bambaataa, 93
Aggressive militarism, 50–52, 55, 60
Agonic activities, 7, 86
American imperialism, 25–26, 136
Amos, 32
Anouar Majid, 39
Anthony Hamilton, 93
Aristotle, 14
Arkoun, Mohamed, 39
Armstrong, Louis, 76, 115
Artistic experiences, 3
Authoritarianism, 24–25, 50, 52, 54–55, 60

B

Badiou, Alain, 4, 114
Baldwin, James, 145
Baraka, Amiri, 80 *see also* LeRoi Jones, 80
Beckett, Samuel, 146
Bernstein, Richard, 107
Black/White opposition, 10
Blues, 3–4, 13–16, 66, 70–83, 88, 94–97, 101, 113–18, 136–38, 142–43, 146–47, 151
Boulad-Ayoub, Josiane, 85
Brothers Karamazov, 58
Brown, James, 14, 78
Bush, George H. W., 104
Bush, George W., 47

C

Chocolate cities, 91–92, 94, 139, 142

Chomsky, Noam, 86
Chraibi, Driss Ferdi, 42
Chuck D, 93
Civil rights, 1, 4, 7–8, 13, 22, 25, 128, 132–33, 135
Clinton, Bill, 5
Coltrane, John, 14, 78, 115
Conceptual persona, 3–4
Constantinian Christianity, 21–23, 26–28, 55, 109, 136, 142
Constantinian hip hop, 92, 94
Contretemps, 81, 89, 137
Cuba, 51
Cultural values, 127, 140

D

Dandyism, 9
Davidson, Donald, 102
Davis, Miles, 14
Debs, Eugène, 126
Deleuze, Gilles, 3, 49
Derrida, Jacques, 4, 6, 102
Dewey, John, 107, 147
Dissonance, 137
Dostoyevsky, Fyodor, 58
Douglass, Frederick, 76
Double consciousness, 91, 128
Dru Hill, 93
Du Bois, W.E.B., 9, 107, 128, 146, 151
Dynamics of capitalism, 22, 45, 120, 142

E

Egypt, 29–30, 32, 38
El-Fadl, Abou, 39
El Saadawi, Nawal, 39
Elites, 124–25, 140–41
Ellington, Duke, 75, 76
Emancipation, 16, 109, 112, 119, 127–28, 136, 142
Emerson, Ralph Waldo, 8
Engagement, 1, 22, 67, 69, 119, 128–30, 136, 139, 145–47, 150
Ethics, 2, 8, 14, 16, 27–28, 31, 55, 69, 97, 107, 137

F

Fanon, Frantz, 15, 127
Foucault, Michel, 4
Franklin, Aretha, 93
Fundamentalism, Christian, 28, 66
Fundamentalism, market, 26, 50, 53–55, 59–60, 92, 125–126
Furious Five, 93

G

Garvey, Marcus, 63
Gaye, Marvin, 14, 78
Grandmaster Flash, 93
Guam, 51

H

Harlem Renaissance, 94–95
Hegel, Georg Wilhelm Friedrich, 14, 147
Hill, Anita, 104–105
Hip hop, 12, 89, 92–94
Hosea, 32
Hughes, Langston, 95

INDEX

I

Imperial Christianity, 26
Inequality, 25, 75, 124
Iran, 38
Isaiah, 32–33,
Isley, Ronald, 93
Israel, 28–36
Israeli-Palestinian Conflict, 31, 33–34

J

Jackson, Jesse, 63, 106
James, William, 107, 151
Jazz, 3–4, 14–16, 70–71, 73–78, 80–83, 94–97, 101, 113–117, 138, 142–143, 151
Jeremiah, 21, 32
Jones, LeRoi, 80, *see also* Baraka, Amiri, 80
Jordanian states, 30

K

Kane, Cheikh Hamidou, 42, 149, 152
Kelly, R., 93
Keys, Alicia, 93
Khomeini, Ayatollah, 38
Kindred, 93
King Jr., Martin Luther, 9, 22, 63, 76, 111, 115, 117, 132, 146
Kool Herc, 93
KRS ONE, 93
Krugman, Paul, 64

L

Lerner, Michael, 34–35,
Levert, Gerald, 93
Lyotard, Jean-François, 102

M

M'Baye, Mariétou, 42
Mahan, Alfred Thayer, 30
McKay, Claude, 95
Mernissi, Fatima, 39
Middle East, 28, 30
Mills, C. Wright, 107
Modern identity, 42
Morrison, Toni, 11, 145

N

Niane, Djibril Tamsir, 14
Nihilism, 44, 46, 50–52, 54–63, 67, 77, 91, 94, 103, 120–21, 123–24, 127–28, 131, 135–36, 141–43, 152

O

Obama, Barack, 5, 26, 51, 63–65
Orality, 87, 113
Outkast, 93–94

P

Palestine, 30, 34–36
Paris, 9, 11, 14, 49, 71, 74, 85, 93, 114, 120, 149–50
Paternalistic nihilism, 50, 57
PATRIOT Act, 46–47, 67–68

Peirce, Charles Sanders, 107
Pendergrass, Teddy, 93
Philippines, 51
Plato, 14
Poetic, 7, 15, 69, 71, 82, 88, 99, 115, 119, 138
Populism, 125
Populist movement, 125
Poverty, 44, 53, 81, 106, 119, 130
Powell, Clayton, 63
Pragmatism, 146–47
Progressive movement, 125
Progressivism, 125
Prophetic Christianity, 21, 23, 25–28, 63, 109–11, 135–36, 142–43, 146
Prophetic pragmatism, 17, 70, 109–110, 112–114, 147
Public Enemy, 93
Puerto Rico, 51
Putnam, Hillary, 102

Q

Quine, WV, 102

R

R&B, 76, 78, 82
Rachjman, John, 102
Racism, 103, 105–6, 111, 146
Rakim, 93
Ramadan, Tariq, 39
Rancière, Jacques, 120
Rap, 4, 74, 76, 82–91, 93, 95, 151
Rawls, John, 8, 108
Reagan, Ronald, 5, 58

Rebel thought, 74
Romantic figure, 17, 116
Rorty, Richard, 102, 107–8
Ruff Endz, 93
Rushdie, Salman, 42
Rhythms, 81, 89, 93, 101, 113, 116
Rhythmic, 80–81

S

Salih, Tayeb, 42
Samoa, 51
Sartre, Jean Paul, 128, 131
Scott, Jill, 93
Sentimental nihilism, 50, 57–59, 141
Slavery, 2, 25, 48–50, 63–64, 79–80, 90, 100, 103, 141, 151
Smith, Bessie, 14, 76
Social movements, 25, 137, 142
Socrates, 117, 123, 150
Socratic questioning, 35, 59, 79, 97, 123, 135
Solidarity, 8, 55, 66, 72, 73, 76, 88, 104, 119, 123, 127, 138–139, 147
Soroush, Abdokarim, 39
Soul, 4, 19, 43, 66, 76, 82, 93, 128, 138
Stiglitz, Joseph, 64
Summers, Lawrence, 12, 85
Supremacists, 7, 48, 61, 74, 95, 103, 109, 121
Symbolic, 7, 45, 77, 79, 81, 85, 87, 89–91, 95–96, 120–23, 140
Symbolic activity, 86

INDEX

T

Taha, Mahmoud Mohamed, 39, 41
The Roots, 93
Theology, 13, 17, 40, 109, 112
Thomas, Clarence, 104
Trade union, 11, 25, 125–26, 142
Tragicomic, 14, 78, 80, 83, 96, 115, 135, 137, 143, 145

U

Union, 11
Universal, 19, 29, 43, 54, 63, 65, 72, 81–82, 99, 109, 117, 128, 130, 141, 143, 152

V

Vandross, Luther, 93
Vanilla suburbs, 142
Vaughan, Sarah, 76

Violence, 1–2, 10, 14–15, 17, 33, 36, 44–50, 52, 54–55, 59, 67–68, 73, 75, 80, 91, 93–94. 103, 106, 120, 122–24, 136, 141, 143
Visible/invisible, 10, 70

W

Washington, Booker T., 63
Watson, Thomas, 126
Wells-Barnett, Ida B., 76
White, Morton, 107
Wilson, Woodrow, 126
Wonder, Stevie, 93

X

X, Malcom, 9, 76

Y

Yourcenar, Marguerite, 15

www.ingramcontent.com/pod-product-compliance
Lightning Source LLC
Chambersburg PA
CBHW032025230426
43671CB00005B/203